TONY BENNETT

ALL TIME GREATEST HITS

T0081888

Photos by Don Hunstein, courtesy of Sony/Columbia Records.

ISBN 978-1-5400-4605-5

Visit Hal Leonard Online at
www.halleonard.com

Contact us:
Hal Leonard
7777 West Bluemound Road
Milwaukee, WI 53213
Email: info@halleonard.com

In Europe, contact:
Hal Leonard Europe Limited
42 Wigmore Street
Marylebone, London, W1U 2RN
Email: info@halleonardeurope.com

In Australia, contact:
Hal Leonard Australia Pty. Ltd.
4 Lentara Court
Cheltenham, Victoria, 3192 Australia
Email: info@halleonard.com.au

THE BEST IS YET TO COME

Music by CY COLEMAN
Lyrics by CAROLYN LEIGH

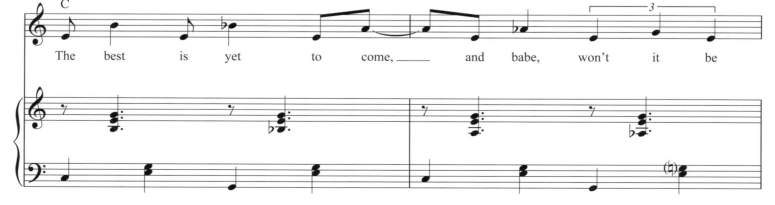

5

fine? ____ The best is yet to come, __

____ come the day you're mine. Come the day you're

mine, ____ I'm gon-na teach you to fly. ___

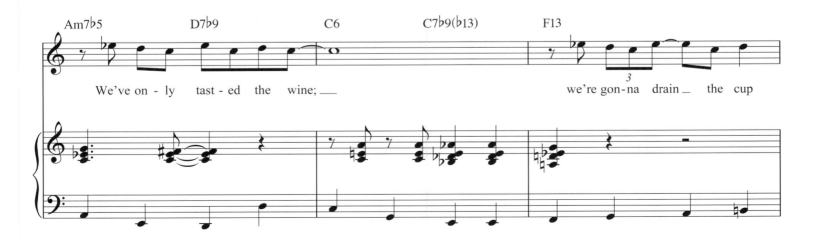

We've on - ly tast - ed the wine; __ we're gon-na drain __ the cup

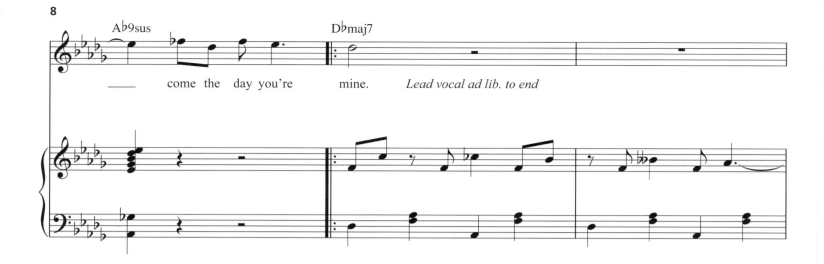

come the day you're mine. *Lead vocal ad lib. to end*

Repeat and Fade

Optional Ending

EVERYBODY'S TALKIN'
(Echoes)

Words and Music by
FRED NEIL

Moderately

skip-ping o - ver the o - cean _____ like a stone.

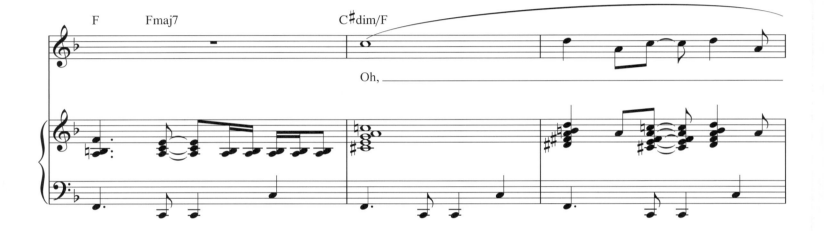

Oh, _____

oh. _____

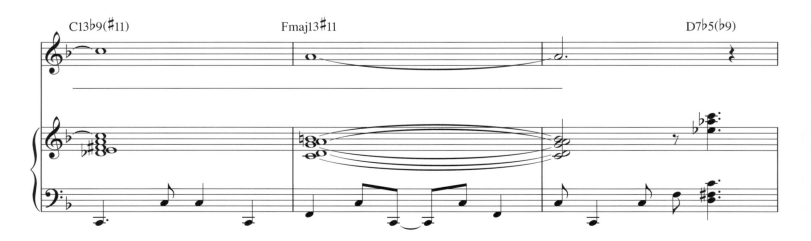

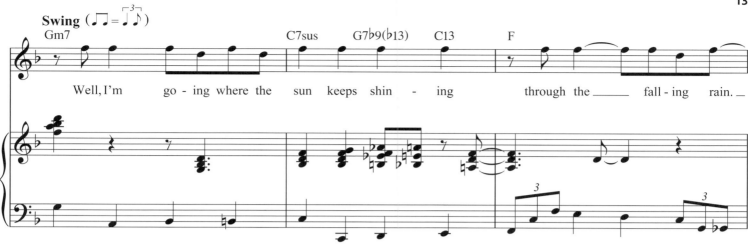

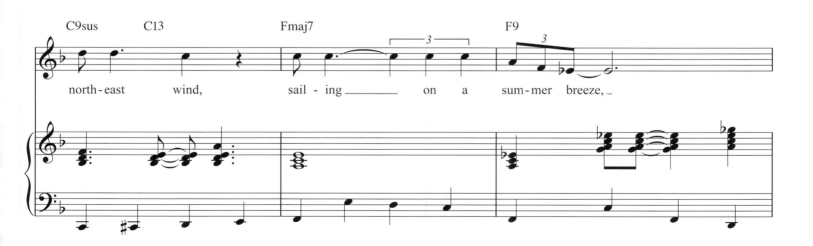

Straight (♫ = ♫)

skip-ping o - ver the o - cean _____ like a stone. _____

Ev - 'ry - bod - y's talk - in' at me. _____ I can't hear a

word they're say - ing; on - ly _____ the ech - oes _____ of my

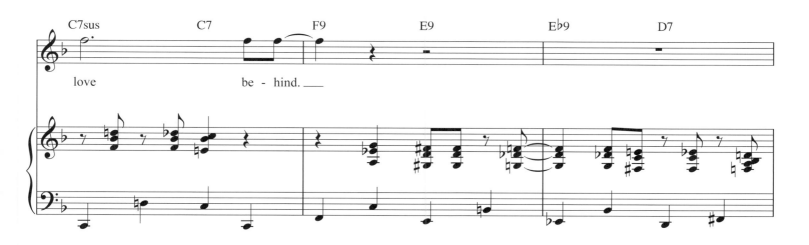

CHEEK TO CHEEK
from the RKO Radio Motion Picture TOP HAT

Words and Music by
IRVING BERLIN

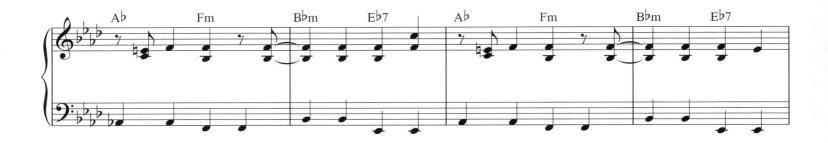

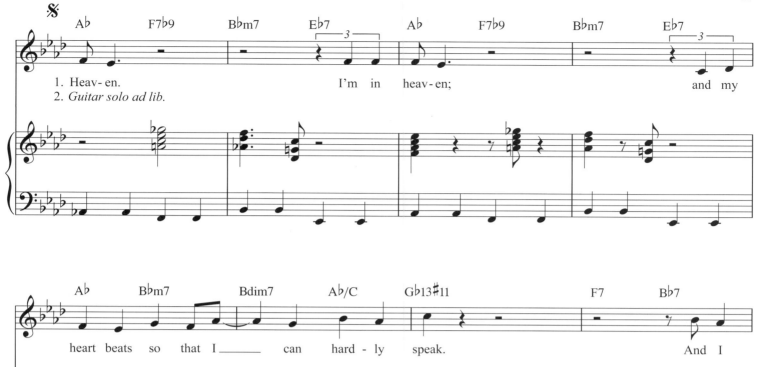

1. Heav- en.
2. *Guitar solo ad lib.*

I'm in heav-en; and my

heart beats so that I _____ can hard - ly speak. And I

seem to find the hap - pi - ness_ I seek when we're

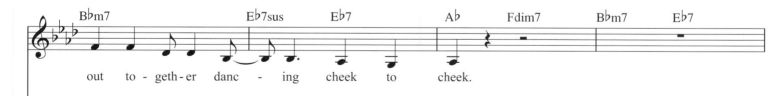

out to - geth- er danc - ing cheek to cheek.

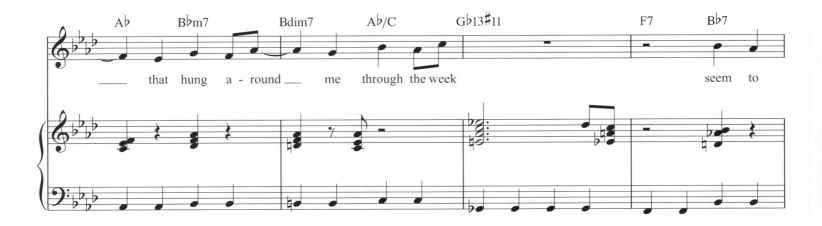

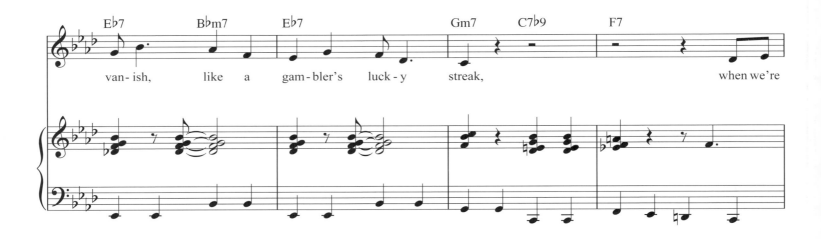

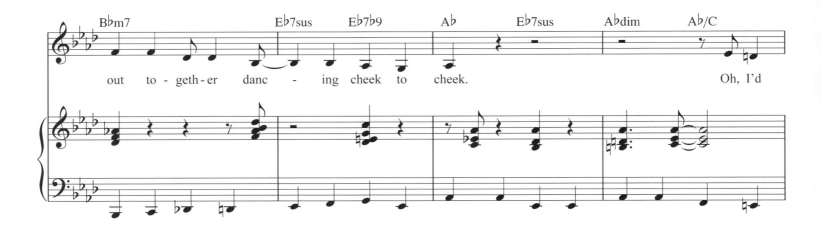

seem to find the ___ hap - pi - ness I seek when we're

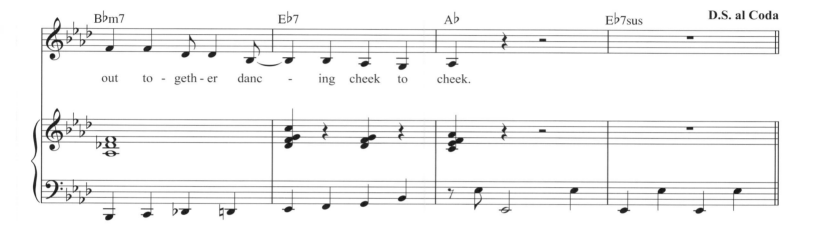

out to - geth - er danc - ing cheek to cheek.

D.S. al Coda

CODA

Dance with me. ___ I want my arm a - bout you. ___ The

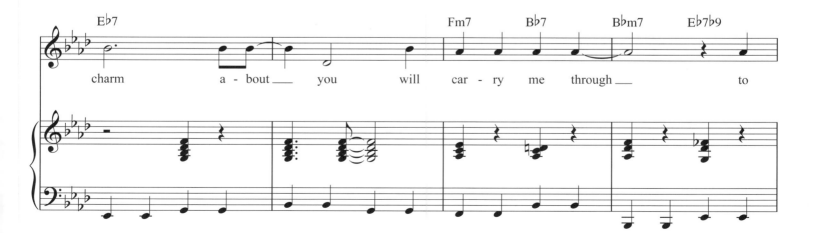

charm a - bout ___ you will car - ry me through ___ to

-ing, out to-geth-er danc - ing cheek to ___

___ cheek.
(2., 3., 4.,...) *Guitar solo ad lib. to end*

Repeat and Fade

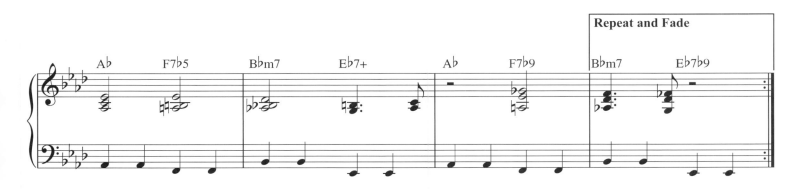

Optional Ending

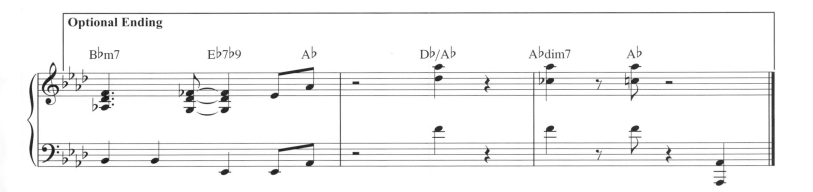

FLY ME TO THE MOON
(In Other Words)

Words and Music by
BART HOWARD

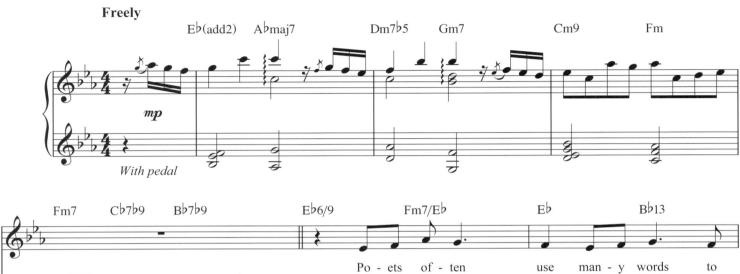

Po-ets of-ten use man-y words to

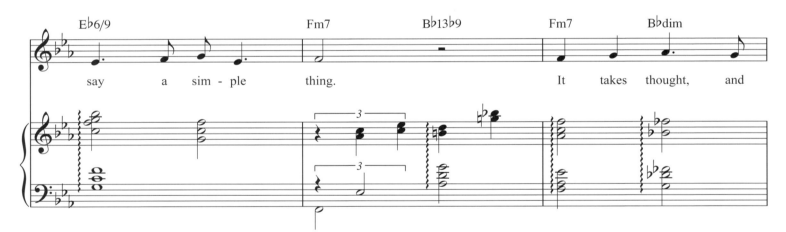

say a sim-ple thing. It takes thought, and

time, and rhyme to make a po-em sing. With

E♭maj9   **A9**   **A♭maj7**   **A♭6**

stars.   Let me see what

Dm7♭5   **G7♭9**   **Cm**   **C7/B♭**

spring   is   like   on Ju-pi-ter   and   Mars."   In

A♭6   **Fm7**   **B♭9sus**   **Dm7♭5/A♭**

oth - er words,   hold   my

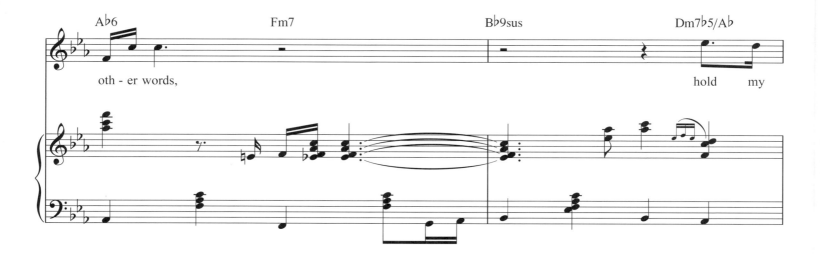

Gm7   **C9**   **C13♭5(♭9)**   **Fm7**

hand.   In oth-er words,

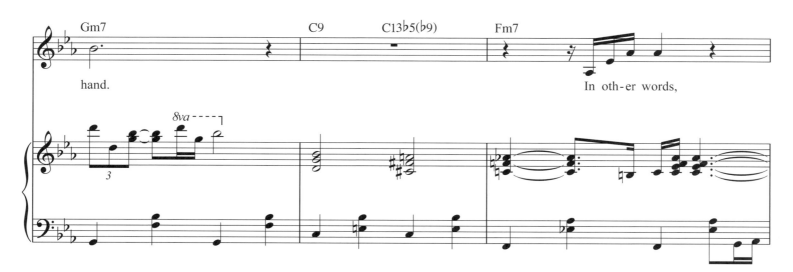

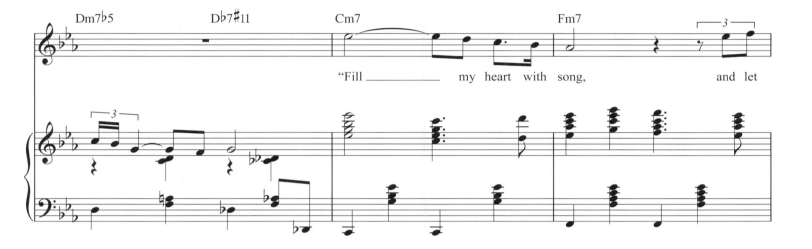

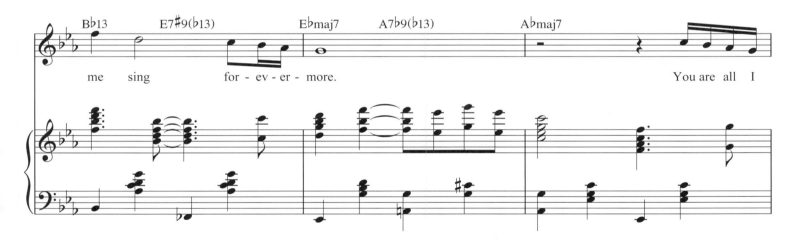

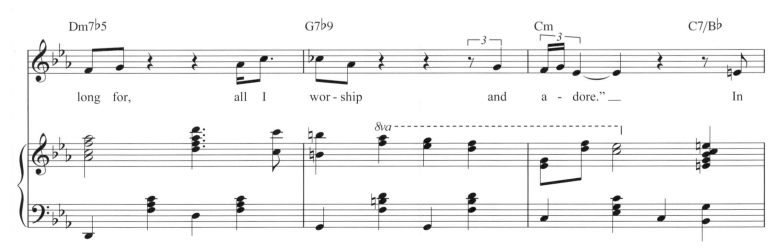

oth-er words, _____ please be true. _____

Slowly, freely

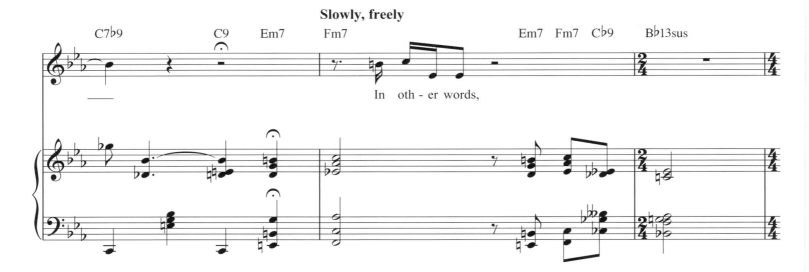

In oth-er words,

I love you.

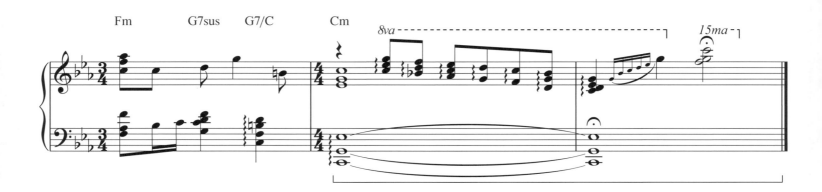

FOR ONCE IN MY LIFE

Words by RONALD MILLER
Music by ORLANDO MURDEN

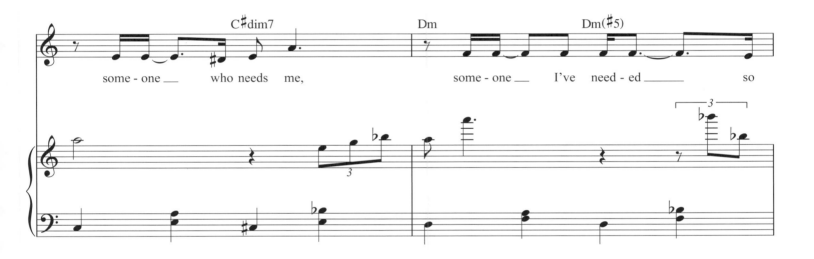

some-how I know I'll be strong. For once, I can touch what my

heart used to dream of _____ long be - fore I

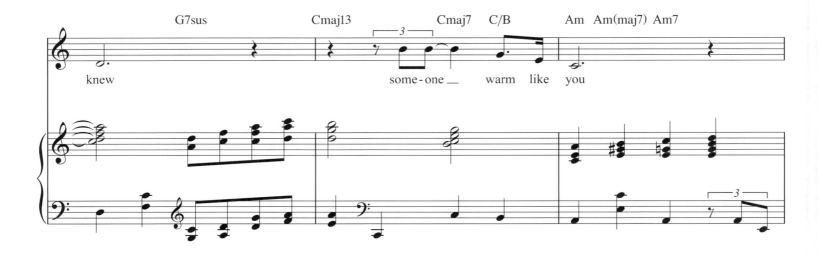

knew some-one __ warm like you would make my dream come

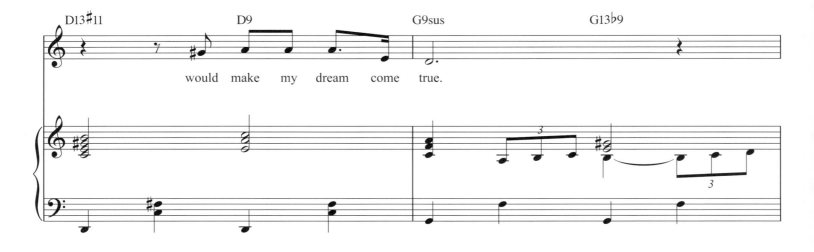

would make my dream come true.

THE GOOD LIFE

Words by JACK REARDON
Music by SACHA DISTEL

hide all the sad-ness you feel. You won't

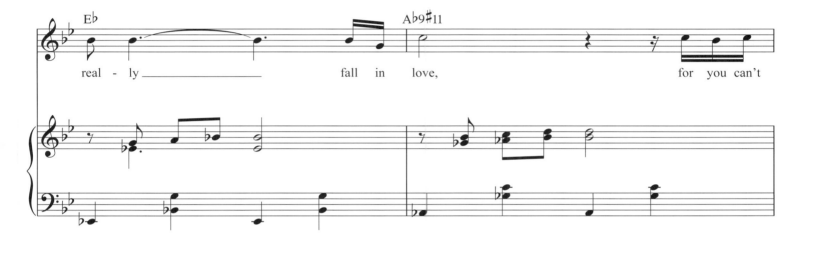

real - ly _____ fall in love, for you can't

take the chance. So please be

hon - est with your - self; don't try to

fake ro-mance. It's the good life; to be

free and ex-plore the un-known, like the

heart-aches when you learn you must face them __ a -

lone. _____ Please re -

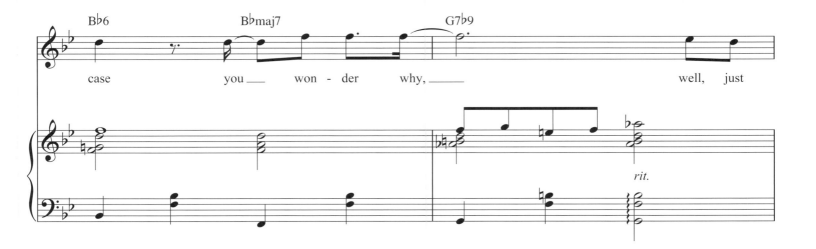

I LEFT MY HEART IN SAN FRANCISCO

Words by DOUGLASS CROSS
Music by GEORGE CORY

The love - li - ness of Par - is seems some - how sad - ly gay. The glo - ry that was Rome is of an - oth - er day. I've been ter - ri - bly a - lone and for-

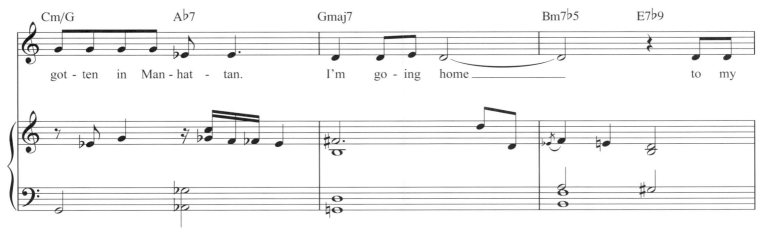

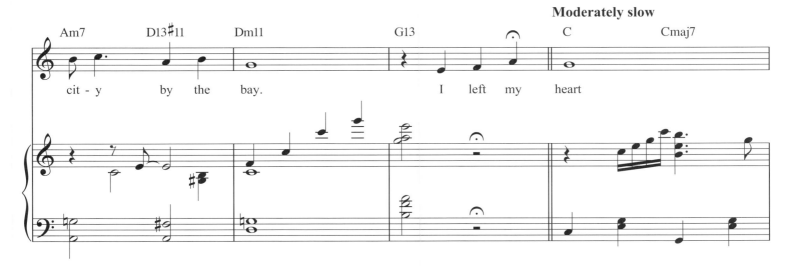

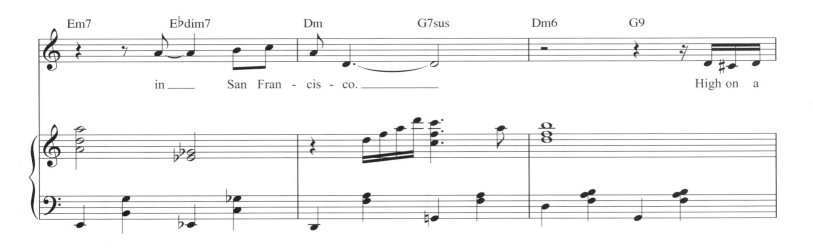

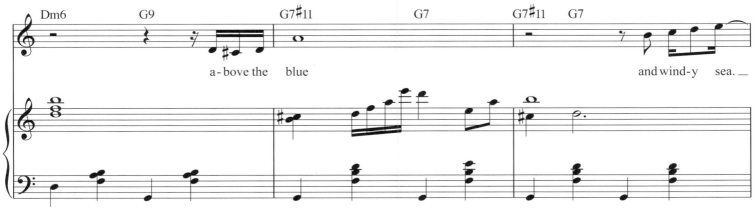

a-bove the blue / and wind-y sea. ___

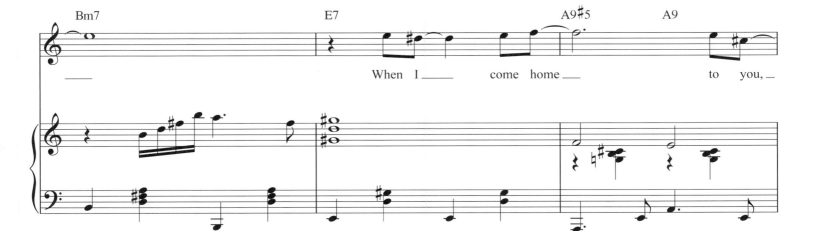

___ When I ___ come home ___ to you, ___

___ San Fran - cis-co, ___ your gold - en

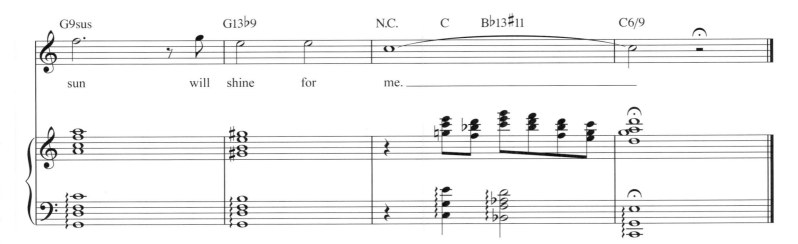

sun will shine for me. _____

I WANNA BE AROUND

Words by JOHNNY MERCER
Music by SADIE VIMMERSTEDT

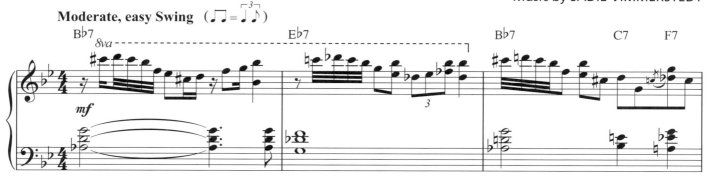

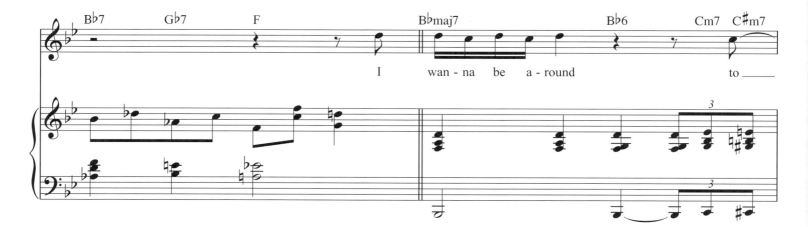

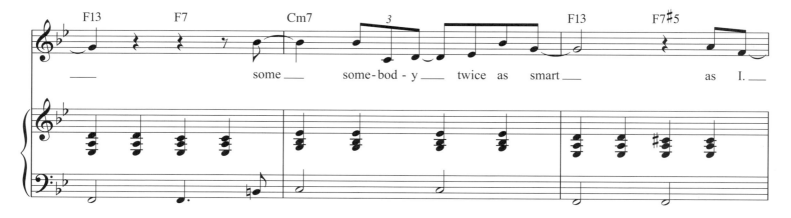

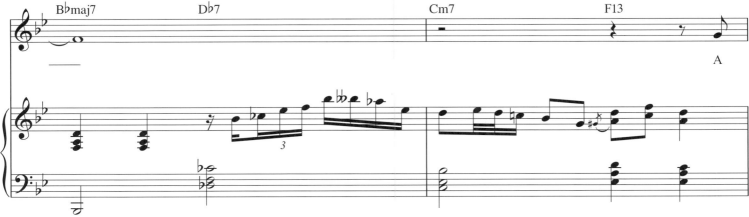

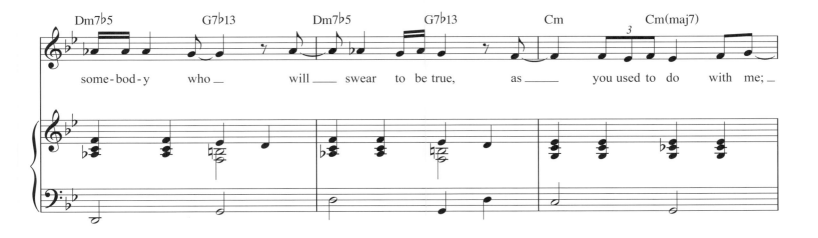

some-bod-y who __ will __ swear to be true, as ____ you used to do with me; __

__ who'll leave you to learn that mis-'ry ____ loves __ com-pa-

ny. Wait and see. I mean, I

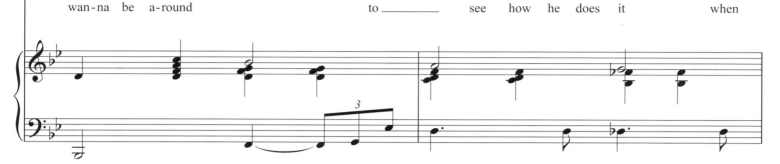

wan-na be a-round to _____ see how he does it when

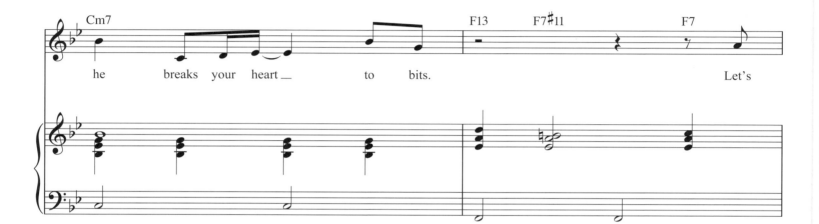

he breaks your heart ___ to bits. Let's

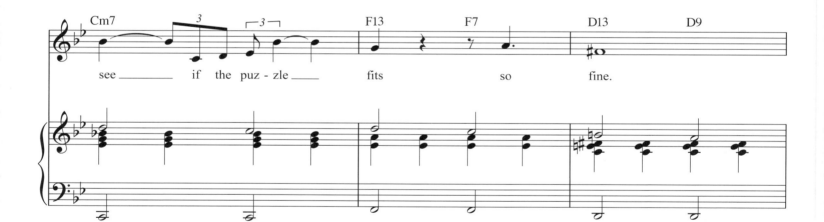

see _____ if the puz - zle _____ fits so fine.

And that's when I'll dis - cov - er that re -

IT HAD TO BE YOU

Words by GUS KAHN
Music by ISHAM JONES

Slowly, very freely

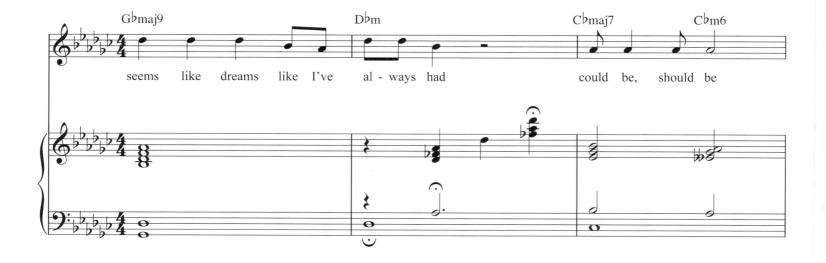

blue, could make me be true;

and e - ven be glad, just to be

sad, think - ing _____ of you. _

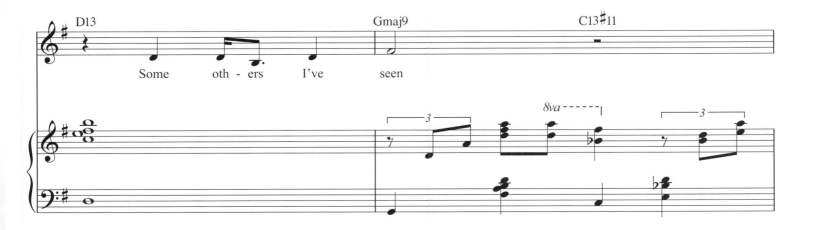

Some oth - ers I've seen

might nev-er be mean,

might nev-er be cross, or try to be boss;

but they would-n't do.

For no-bod-y else gave me a

JUST IN TIME

from BELLS ARE RINGING

Words by BETTY COMDEN and ADOLPH GREEN
Music by JULE STYNE

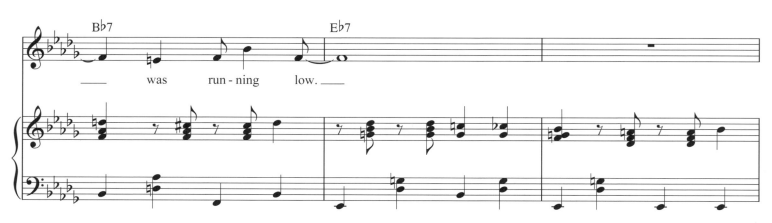

doubt or fear: I've found my way,

for love came just in time. You ___ found me ___

___ just in time, ___ and ___ changed my ___ lone - ly life that ___

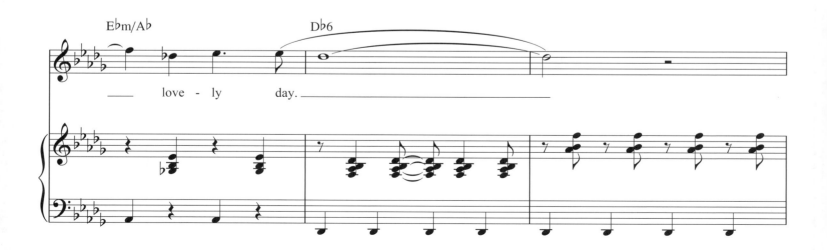

___ love - ly day. ___

Mm, I was lost;

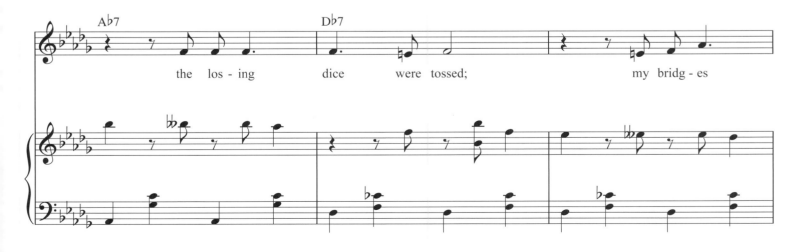

the los - ing dice were tossed; my bridg - es

all were crossed: no - where to go.

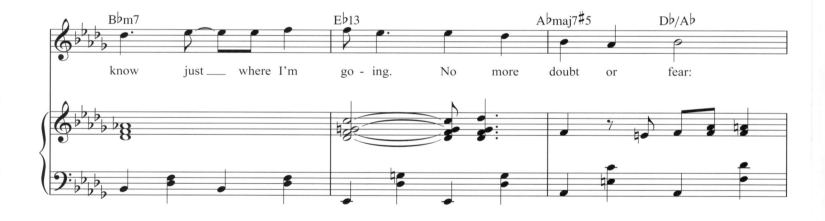

Now you're here, and now I

know just where I'm go - ing. No more doubt or fear:

I've found my way, for love came

just in time. You found me just in time, ___

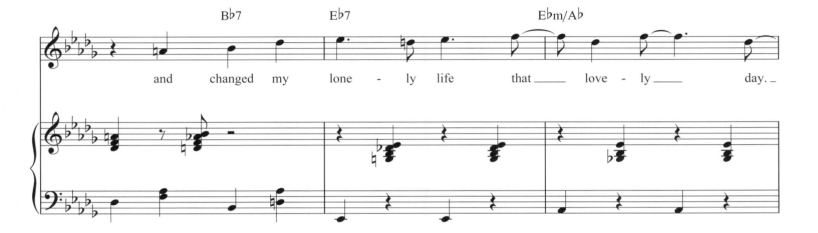

and changed my lone - ly life that ___ love - ly ___ day. ___

NIGHT AND DAY

Words and Music by
COLE PORTER

Fast Swing

Like the beat, beat, beat of the tom - tom when the

jun - gle shad - ows fall; ___ like the tick, tick, tock of the state - ly clock ___ as it ___

___ stands a - gainst the wall; ___ like the ___ like the

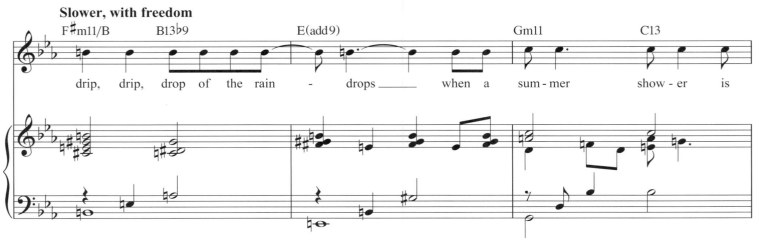

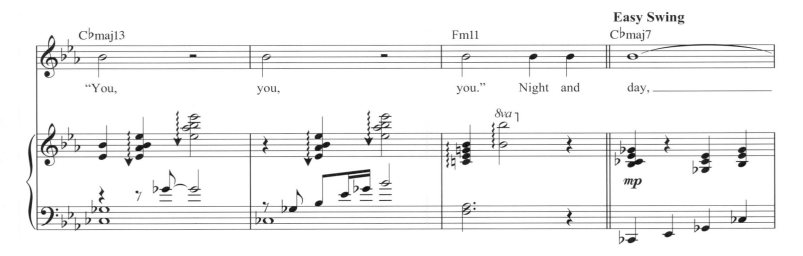

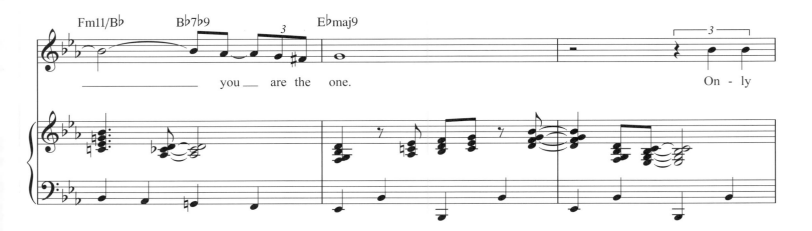

you be-neath the moon and un-der the sun. ___

Wheth-er near to me ___ or far, it's

no mat-ter, dar - ling, ___ where you are. I _____ think of you

night and day. ___ Day and night,

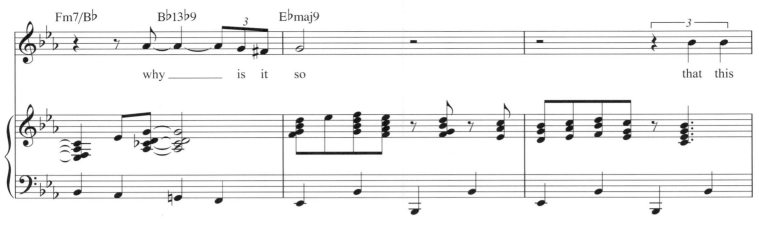

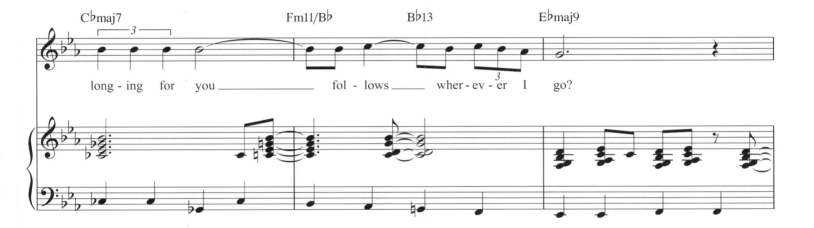

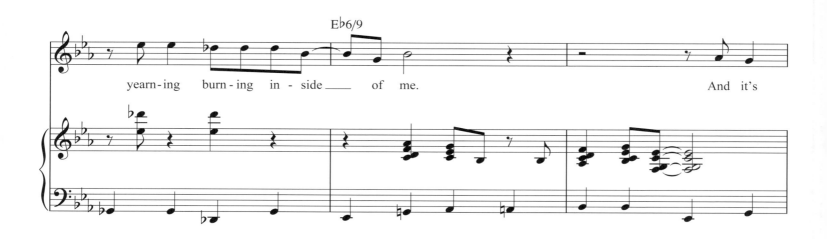

life mak-ing love to you day and night, night and

day. *Piano Solo ad lib.*

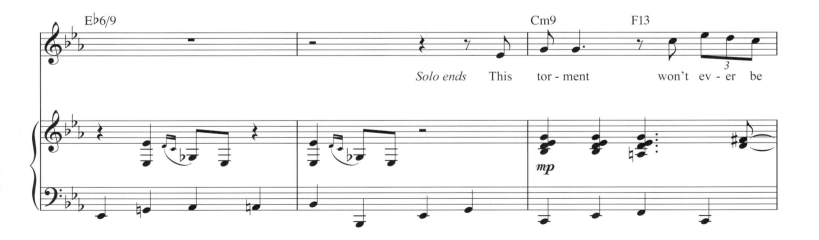

Solo ends This tor-ment won't ev-er be

ONE FOR MY BABY
(And One More for the Road)

Lyric by JOHNNY MERCER
Music by HAROLD ARLEN

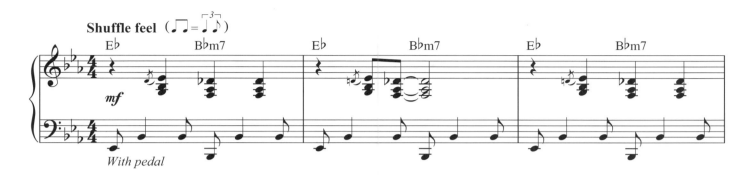

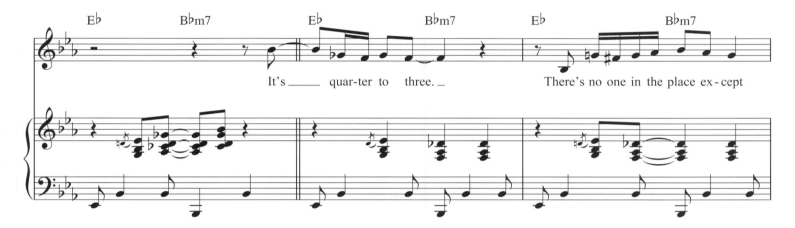

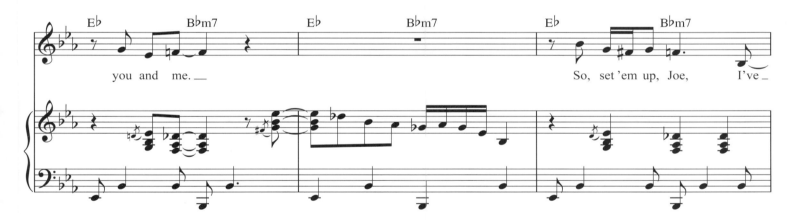

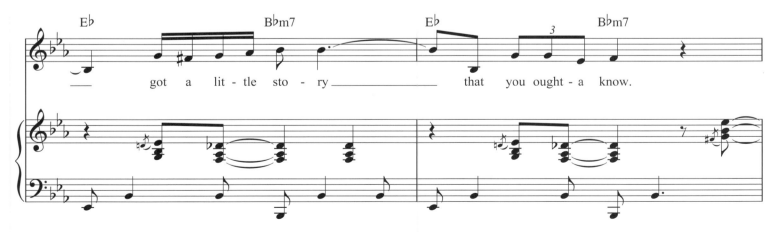

We're drink-ing, my friend, to the end of a brief __ ep - i - sode. Make it one __ for my __ ba - by, __ and one __ more for __ the road. __ I've __

__ got the rou - tine: __ drop an - oth - er nick - el __

in the ma-chine. *(Spoken:) Nickel?! Oh, gosh!* I'm ____ feel-ing so bad; ____ I

wish you'd make the mu- sic dream - y and sad. ____

I could tell you a lot, but you've got - ta be ____ true ____

____ to your code. ____ So, make it one for my ba - by, and ____

That's how it goes. ___ Joe, ___ I know you're get-ting

D.S. *Spoken Vocal ad lib.*

anx-ious to close. ___ So, thanks for the cheer. ___

Instrumental Solo ad lib.

I hope you did-n't mind my ___ bend-ing your ___ ear. ___ This torch ___

___ that I've found must ___ be drowned, or it soon ___ might ex - plode. ___

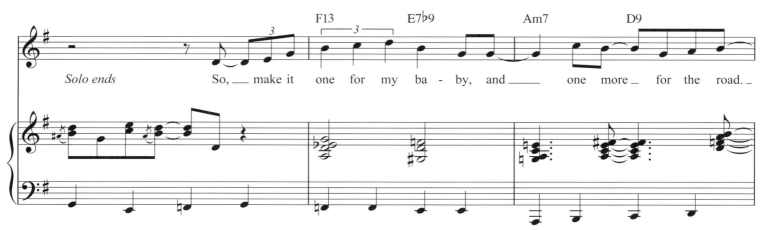

Solo ends So, ___ make it one for my ba - by, and ___ one more ___ for the road. ___

To Coda ⊕

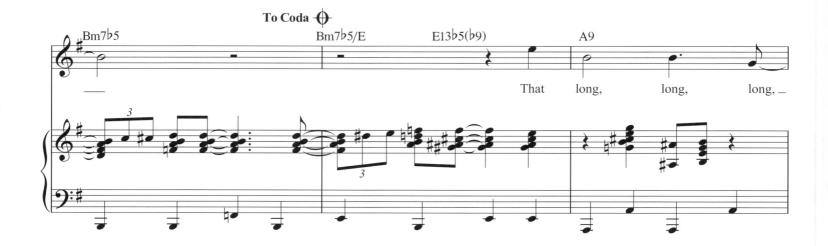

___ That long, long, long, ___

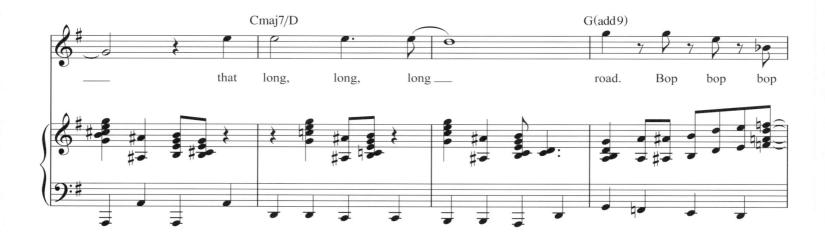

___ that long, long, long ___ road. Bop bop bop

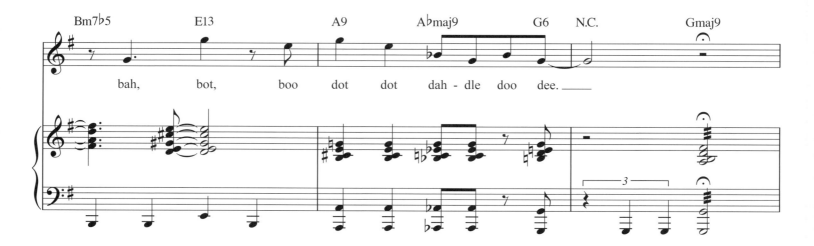

bah, bot, boo dot dot dah - dle doo dee. ___

PUT ON A HAPPY FACE
from BYE BYE BIRDIE

Lyric by LEE ADAMS
Music by CHARLES STROUSE

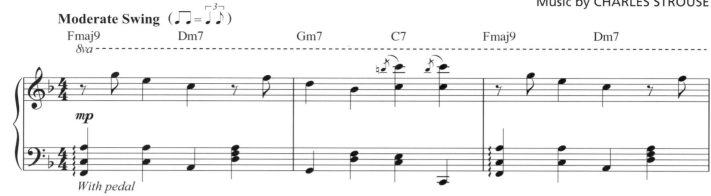

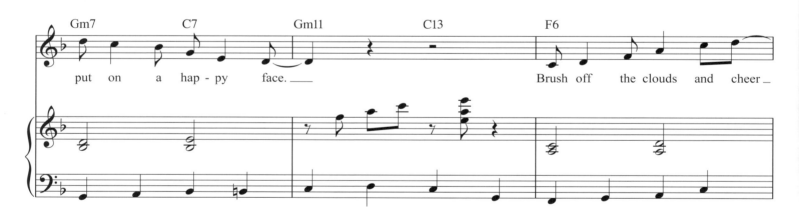

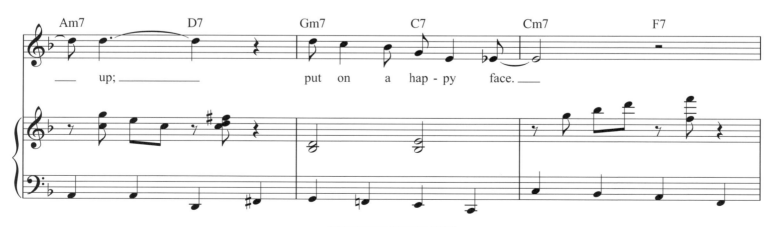

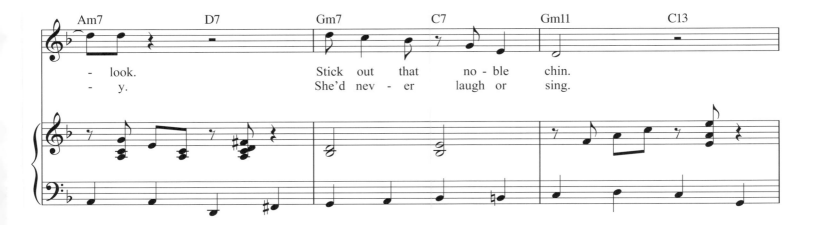

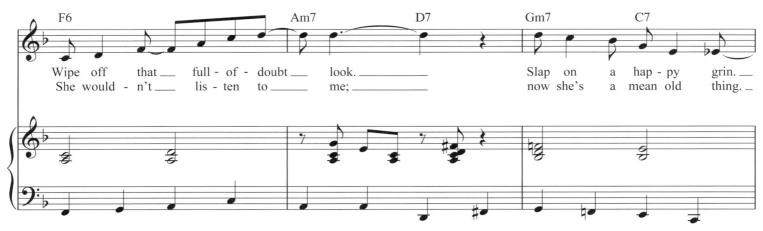

Wipe off that __ full - of - doubt __ look. _____ Slap on a hap - py grin. __
She would - n't __ lis - ten to _____ me; _____ now she's a mean old thing. __

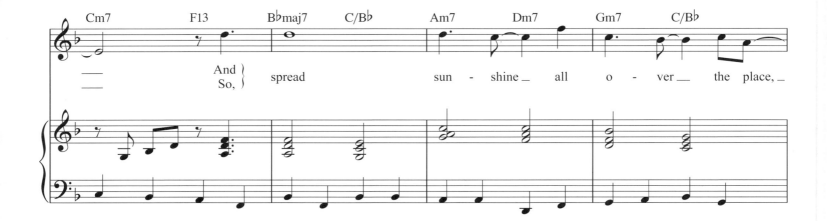

__ And ⎫ spread sun - shine __ all o - ver __ the place, __
So, ⎭

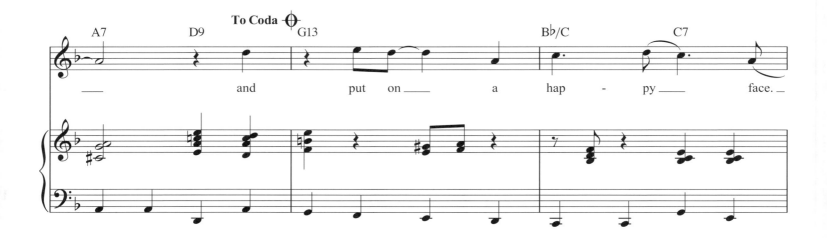

__ and put on __ a hap - py __ face. __

To Coda ⊕

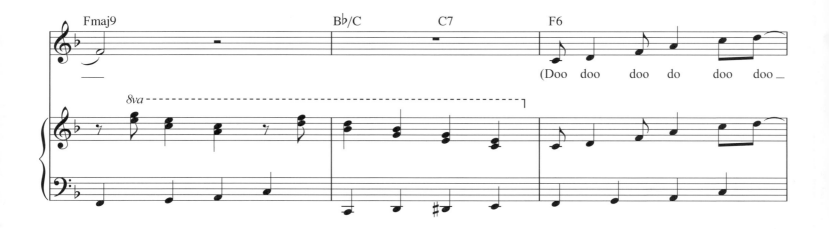

__ (Doo doo doo do doo doo __

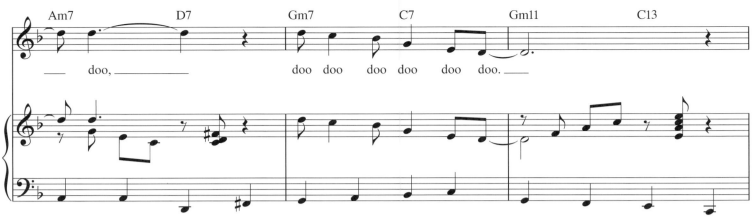

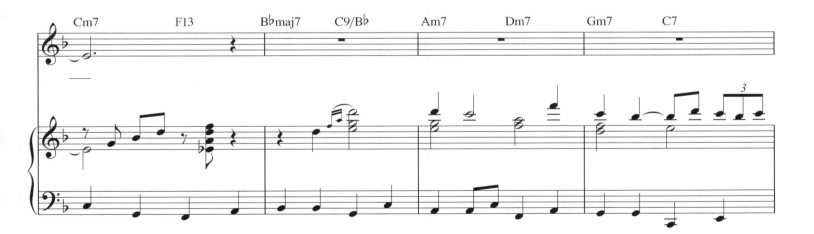

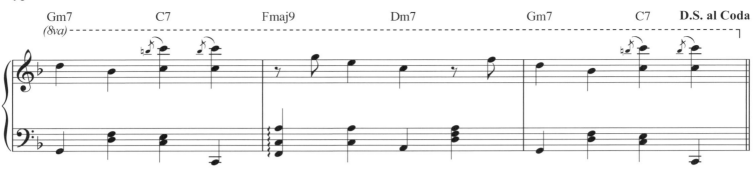

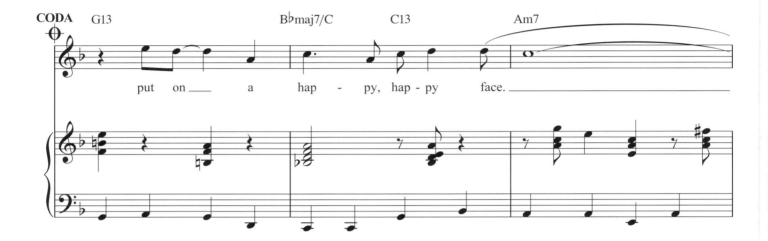

put on ___ a hap - py, hap - py face. ___

___ Put on ___ a hap - py, hap - py, hap - py

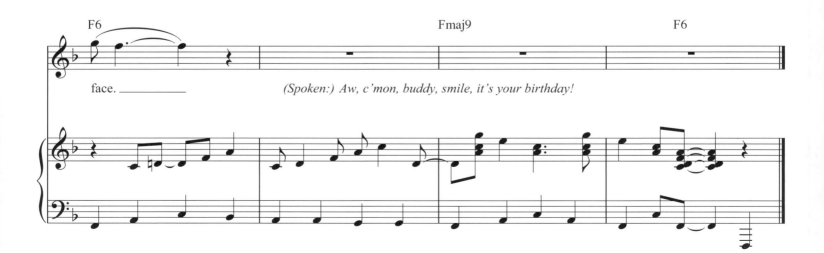

face. ___

(Spoken:) Aw, c'mon, buddy, smile, it's your birthday!

A RAINY DAY

Words by HOWARD DIETZ
Music by ARTHUR SCHWARTZ

Moderate Swing

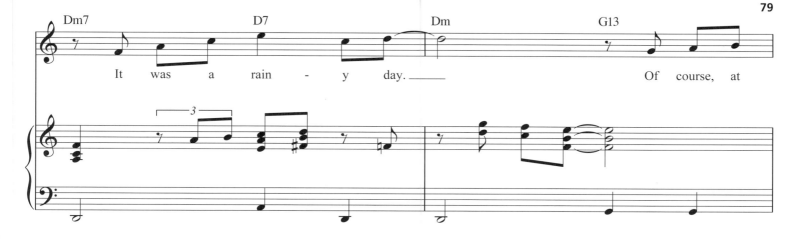

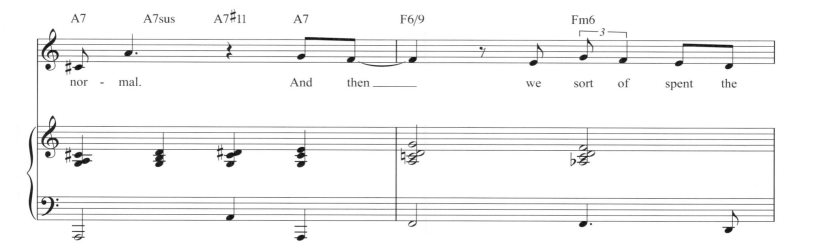

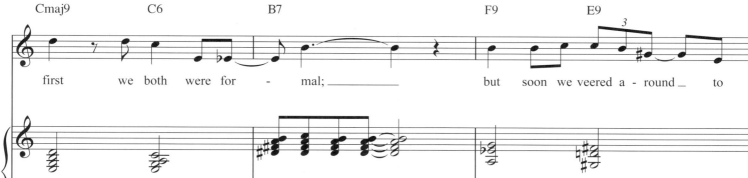

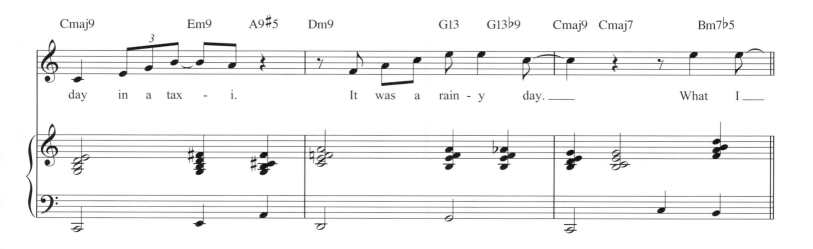

RAGS TO RICHES

Words and Music by RICHARD ADLER
and JERRY ROSS

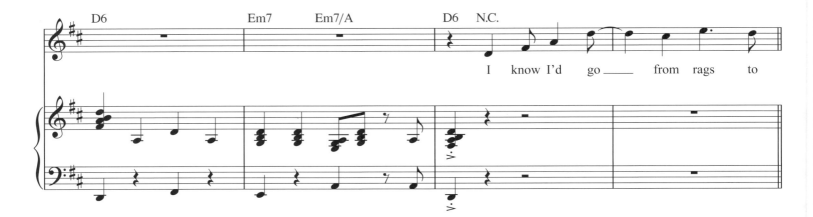

I know I'd go ___ from rags to

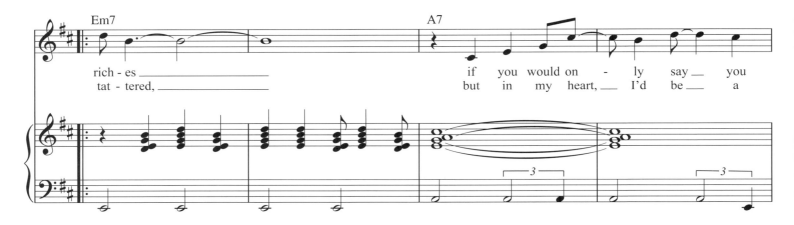

rich - es ___ if you would on - ly say ___ you

tat - tered, ___ but in my heart, ___ I'd be ___ a

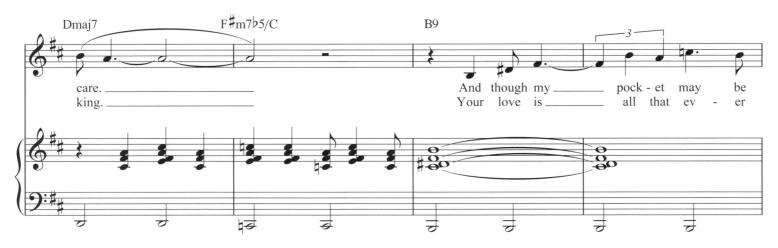

care. ___ And though my ___ pock - et may be

king. ___ Your love is ___ all that ev - er

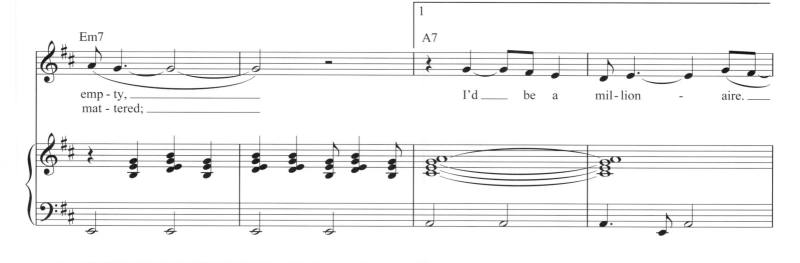

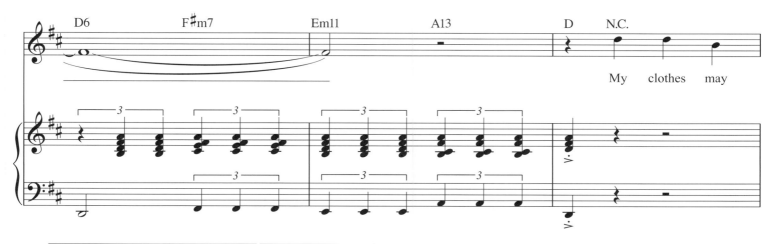

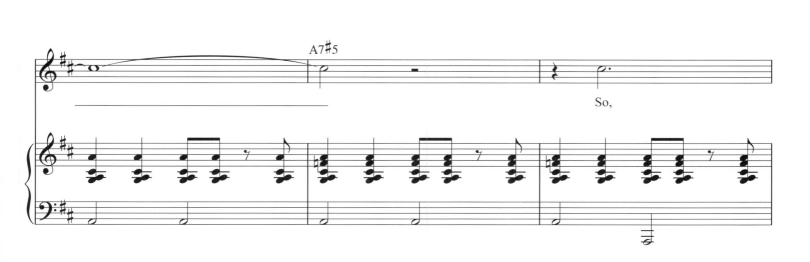

o - pen __ your arms, and you'll o - pen __ the door __

__ to ev - 'ry __ treas - ure __ that

I'm hop - ing for. __ Hold me and

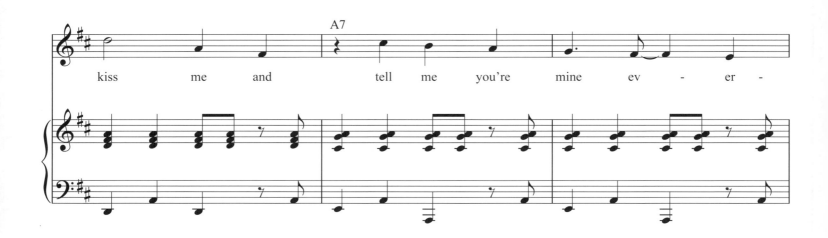

kiss me and tell me you're mine ev - er -

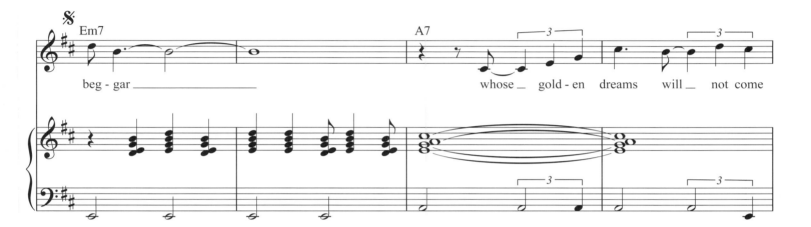

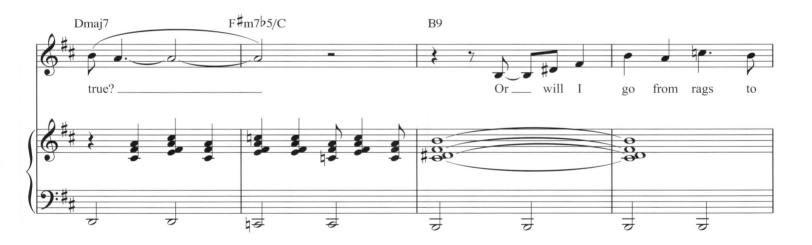

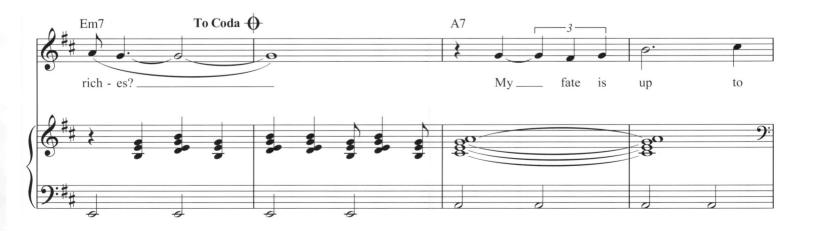

you.

Instrumental solo

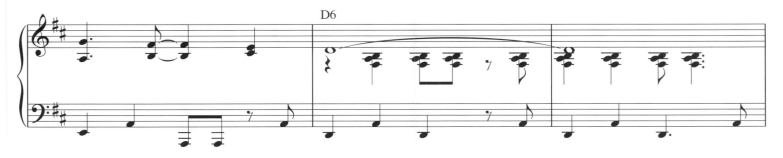

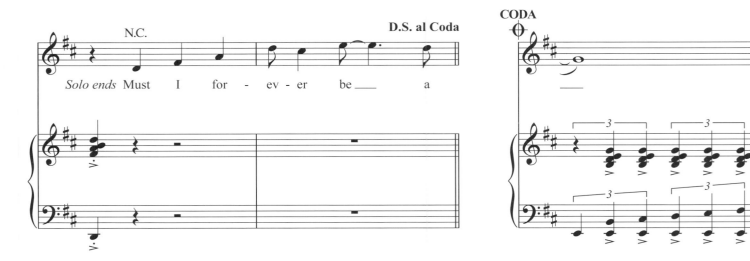

D.S. al Coda

CODA

Solo ends Must I for - ev - er be ___ a

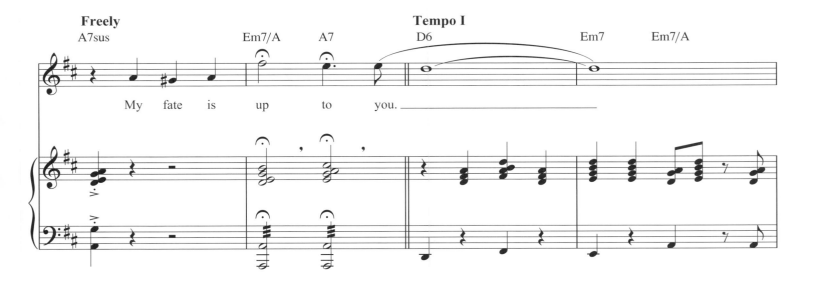

Freely

Tempo I

A7sus   Em7/A   A7   D6   Em7   Em7/A

My fate is up to you. ___

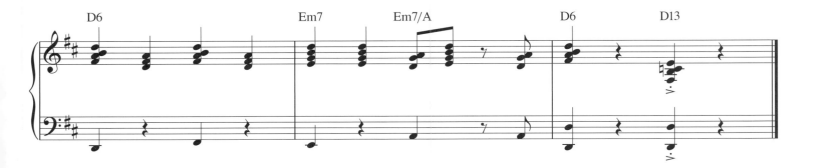

D6   Em7   Em7/A   D6   D13

SING, YOU SINNERS

`Theme from the Paramount Picture SING, YOU SINNERS

Words and Music by SAM COSLOW
and W. FRANKE HARLING

ev-'ry-thing, let the har-mo-ny ring up to

heav-en. *Both:* Sing, __ you sin-ners! *Vocal 2:* Just wave your

arms all a-bout, __ let the Lord hear you shout. __ Pour the

mu-sic right out. _____ Sing, __ you sin-ners! _____

F#7#5(b9)　　B7#5(b9)　　Em13　　　　　Em6　　　Am(add9)　　Gm13

Vocal 1: When - ev - er there's mu - sic,

F#m11b5　　F13　　Em6　Bm7(add11)　Em6　　　　　　　E7#5(#9)

the dev - il kicks! He don't al - low mu - sic ___

A13#11　　　　　　　D(add9)　N.C.　　　Gmaj7　　　G6

by the Riv - er Styx. ___ *Vocal 2:* You're wick - ed and you're de - praved ___

Gmaj7　　G6　　Gm7　　C9　　　Gm7　　C9　　Bm7　　E7

___ and you've all mis - be - haved. ___ If you wan-na be saved,

sing, __ you sin - ners! __ *Vocal 1 (Spoken): Well, up until now,*

we've been asking everybody to sing. *But if you won't sing,* *c'mon, dance!*

Go, band! Swing! Go!

Yeah! Swing,

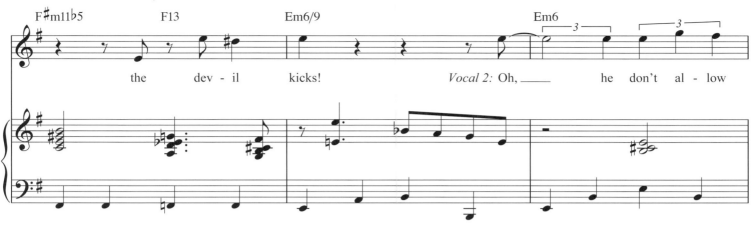

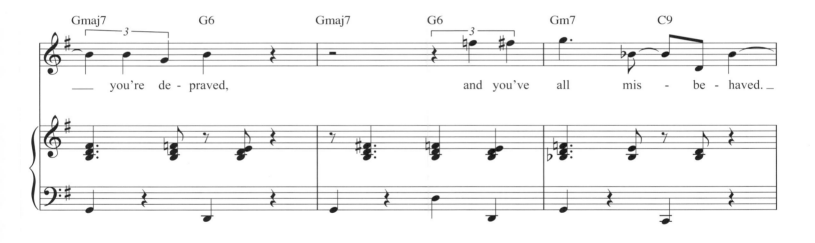

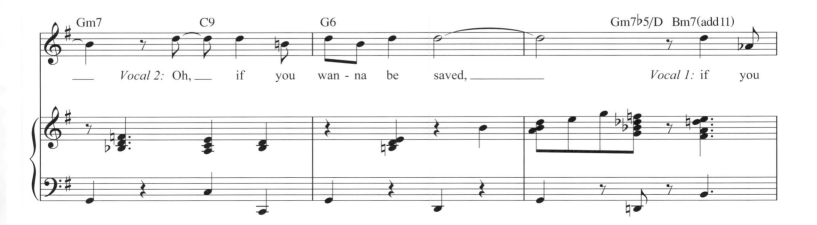

wan - na be saved, _____ *Both:* well, sing,

you sin - ners! _____

Vocal 1: Bop bop bah, ___

bop bop bah, ___ bah bo bah bo bah bop bo dey!

SOMETHING

Words and Music by
GEORGE HARRISON

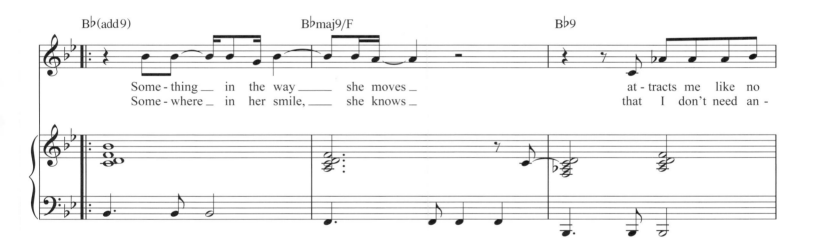

Some-thing __ in the way _____ she moves __ at-tracts me like no
Some-where __ in her smile, _____ she knows __ that I don't need an-

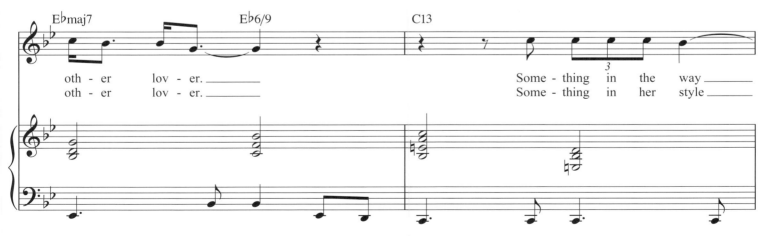

oth-er lov-er. _____
oth-er lov-er. _____ Some-thing in the way _____
Some-thing in her style _____

she woos _____ me. ⎫
that shows _____ me. ⎬ I don't wan-na leave ___ her now. _____

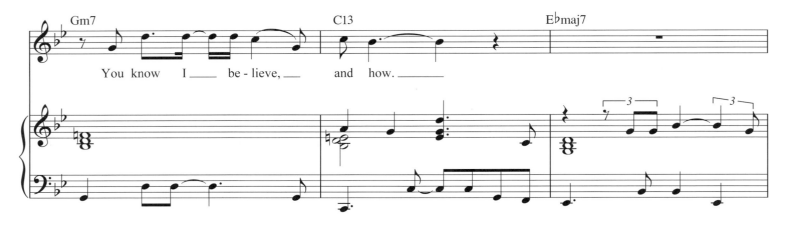

You know I ____ be - lieve, ____ and how. ____

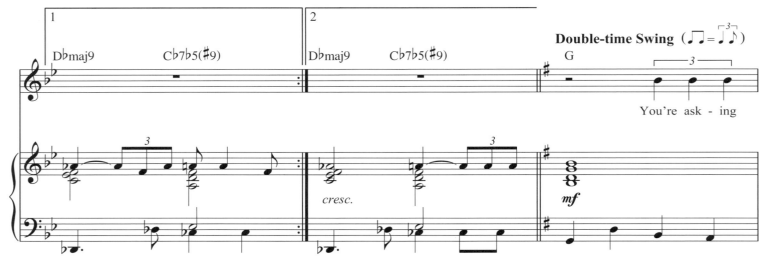

You're ask - ing

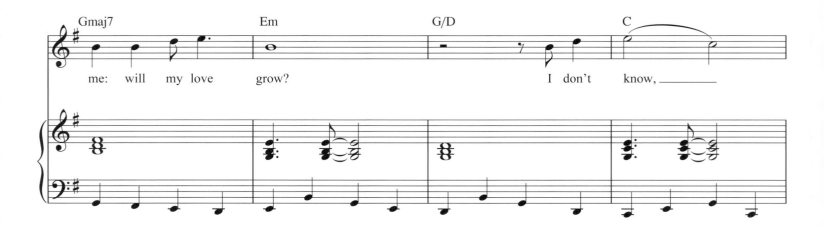

me: will my love grow? I don't know, _____

Double-time Swing

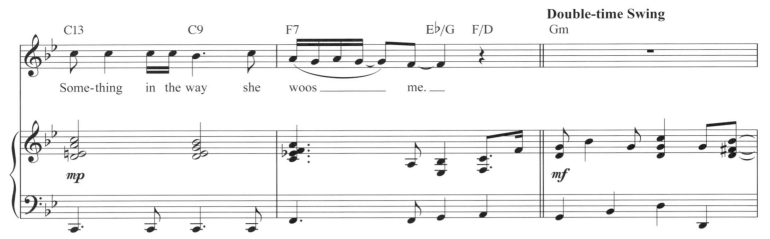

Some-thing in the way she woos _____ me. __

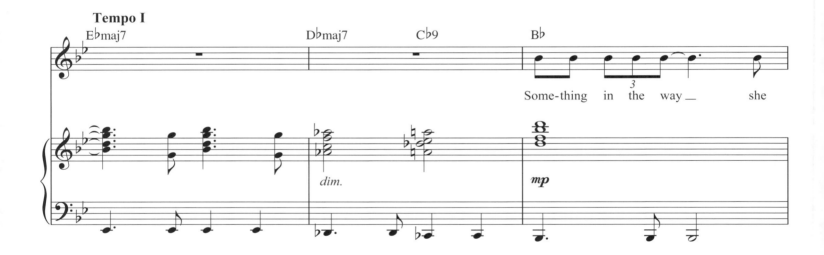

Tempo I

Some-thing in the way __ she

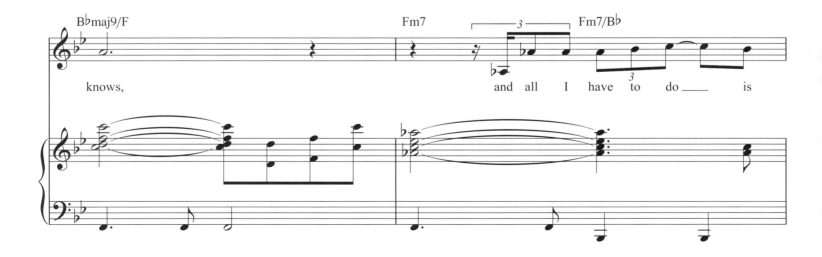

knows, and all I have to do __ is

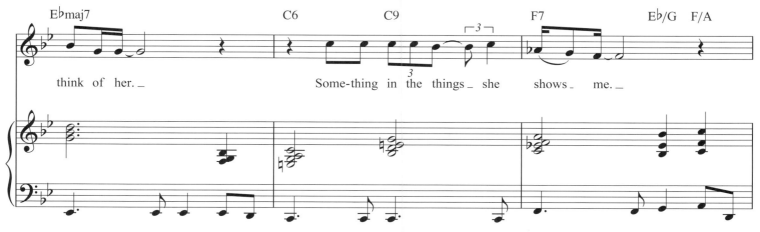

think of her. _

Some-thing in the things _ she shows _ me. _

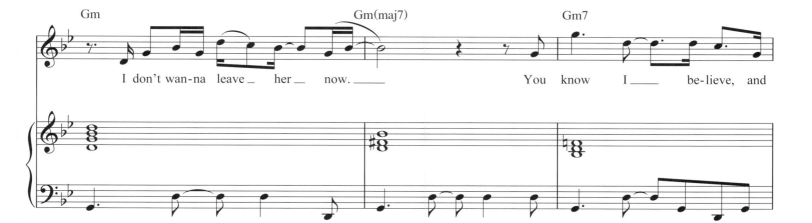

I don't wan-na leave _ her _ now. _

You know I _ be-lieve, and

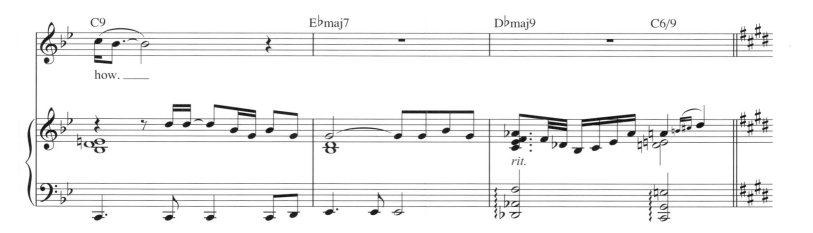

how. _

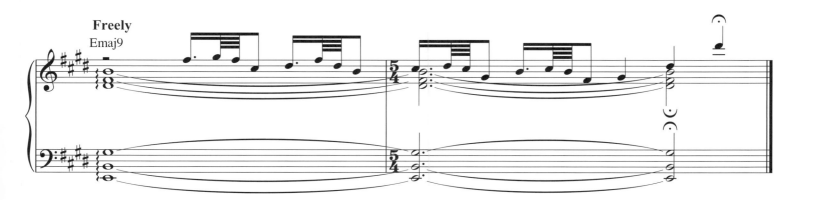

SMILE

Words by JOHN TURNER
and GEOFFREY PARSONS
Music by CHARLES CHAPLIN

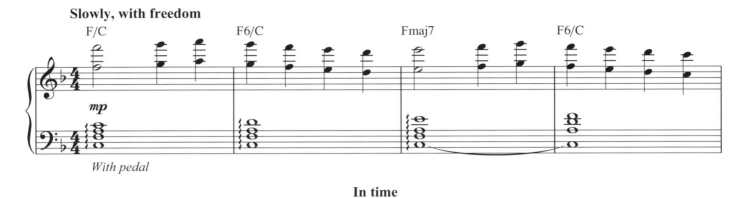

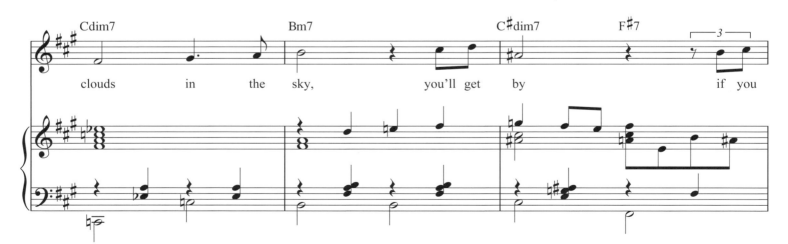

smile _____ through your fear and sor-row. Smile, _____ and may-

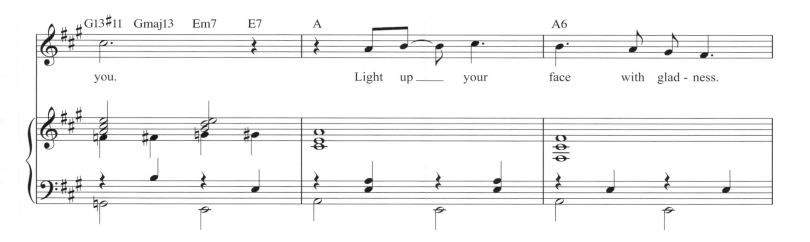

be to-mor-row you'll see the sun come shin-ing through for

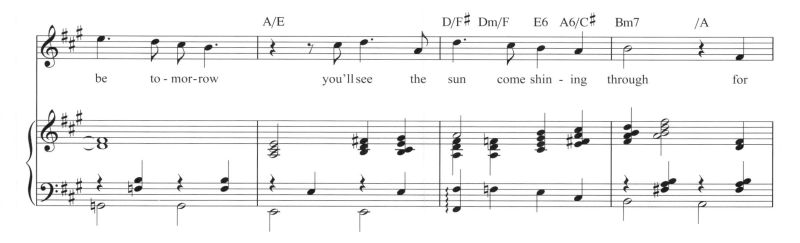

you. Light up ___ your face with glad - ness.

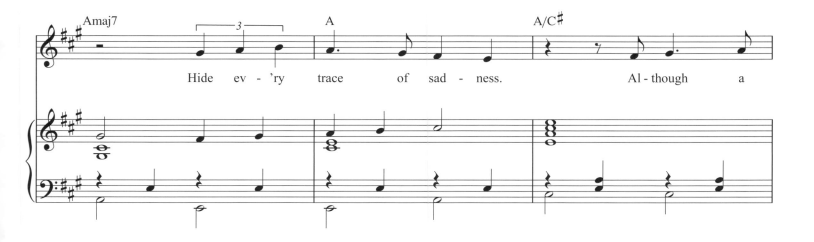

Hide ev - 'ry trace of sad - ness. Al - though a

tear _____ may be ev - er _____ so _____ near, _____ that's the

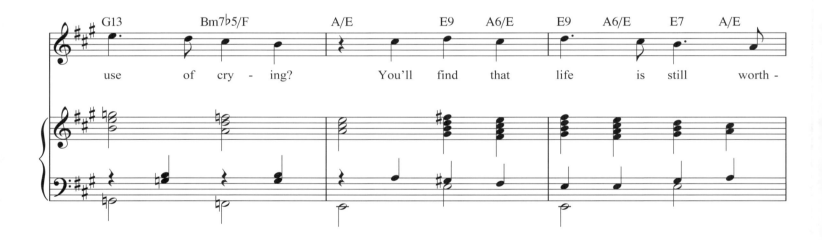

time _____ you must keep on try - ing. _____ Smile; _____ what's the

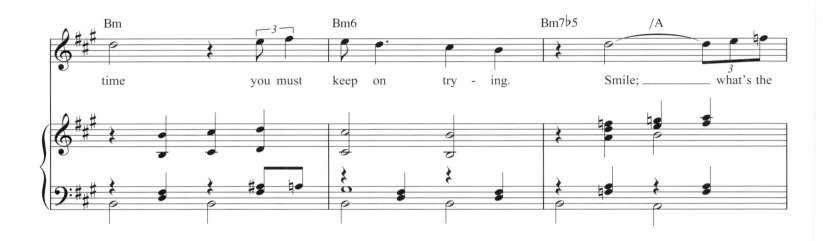

use of cry - ing? _____ You'll find that life is still worth -

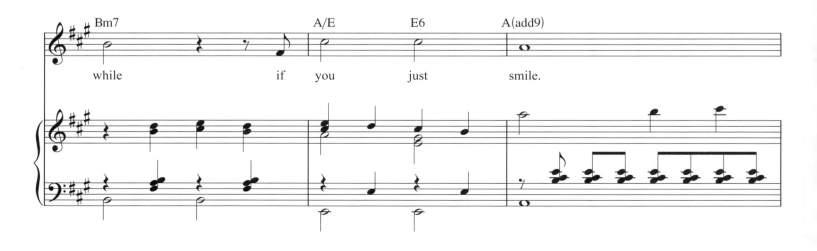

while _____ if you just smile.

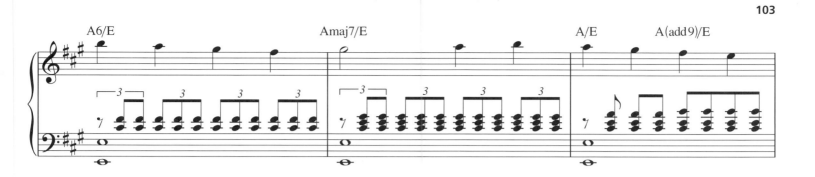

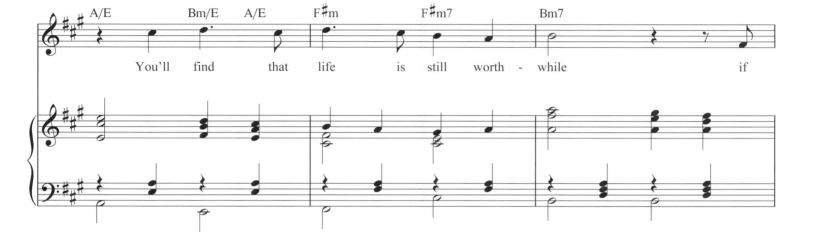

You'll find that life is still worth - while if

Freely, moving faster

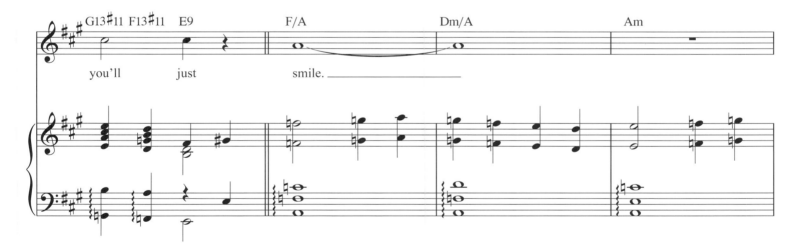

you'll just smile.

STEPPIN' OUT WITH MY BABY

from the Motion Picture Irving Berlin's EASTER PARADE

Words and Music by
IRVING BERLIN

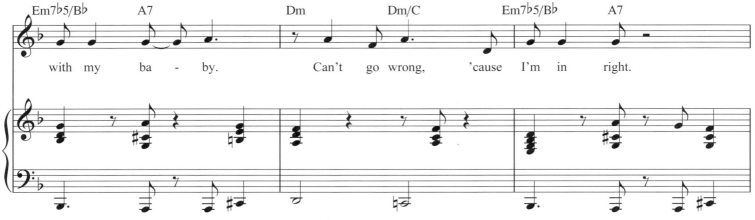

with my ba - by. Can't go wrong, 'cause I'm in right.

To Coda ⊕

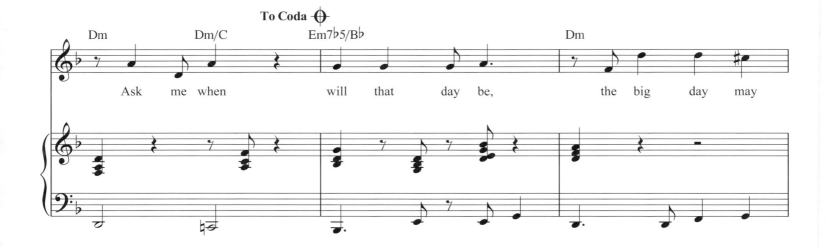

Ask me when will that day be, the big day may

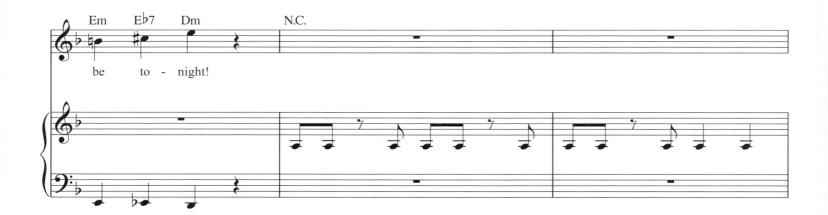

be to - night!

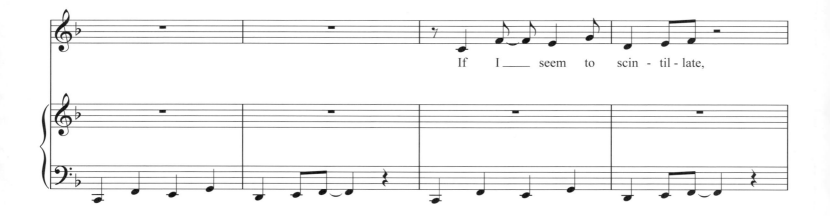

If I ___ seem to scin - til - late,

why   I   feel   sub - lime...   Dance!

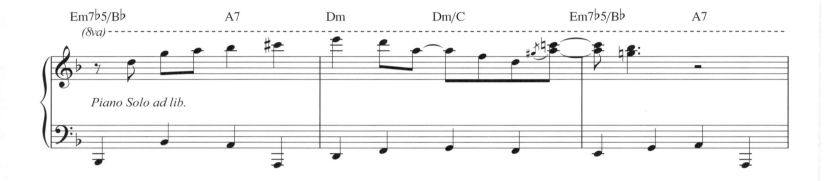

Piano Solo ad lib.

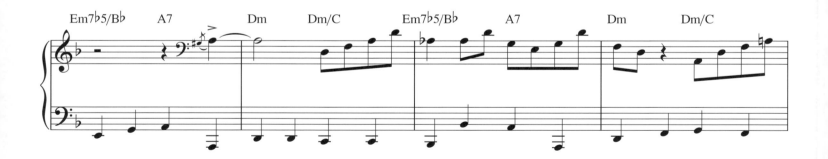

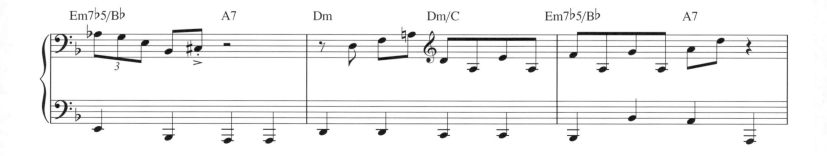

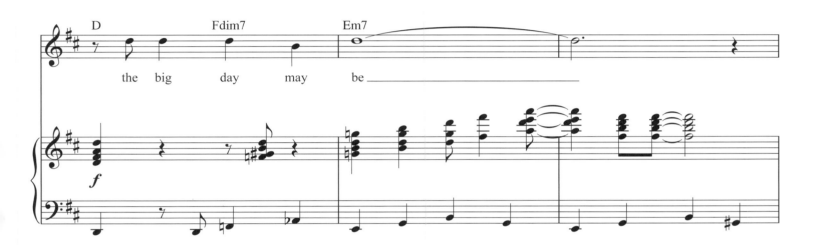

STRANGER IN PARADISE
from KISMET

Words and Music by ROBERT WRIGHT
and GEORGE FORREST
(Music Based on Themes of A. BORODIN)

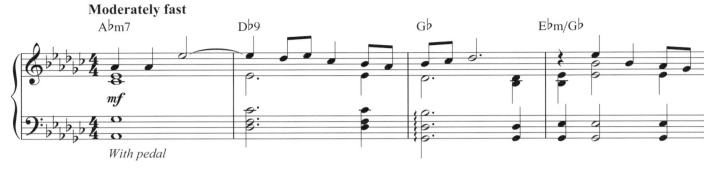

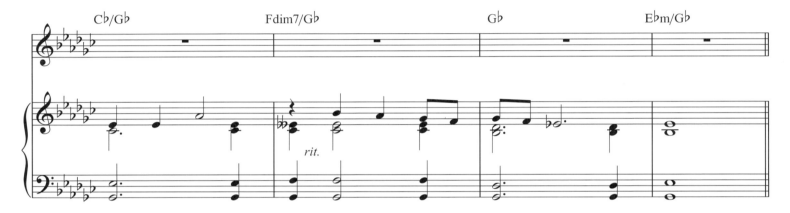

Take my hand, ____ I'm ____ a stran-ger in par-a-dise, ____ oh, lost in a

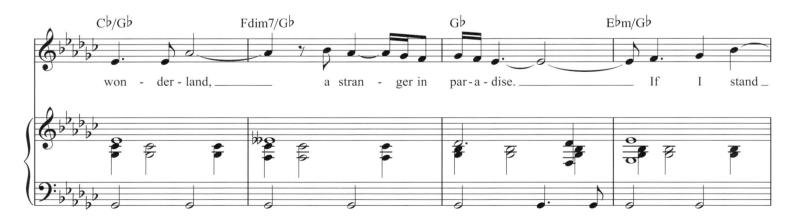

won-der-land, ____ a stran-ger in par-a-dise. ____ If I stand ____

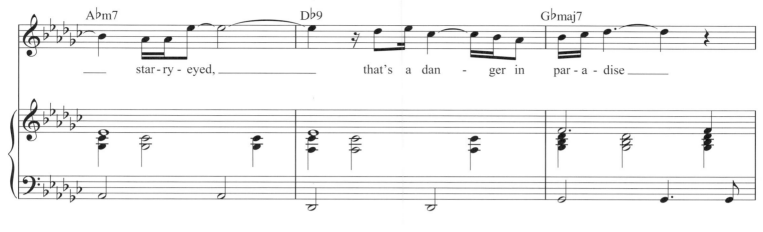

star-ry - eyed, _____ that's a dan - ger in par - a - dise _____

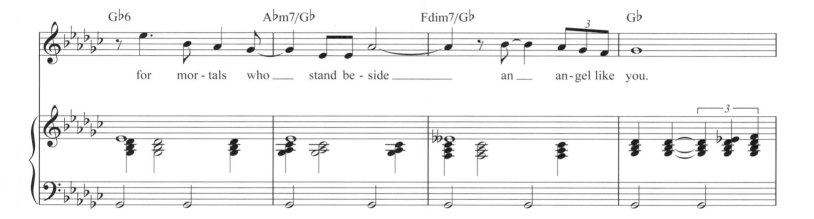

for mor-tals who ___ stand be - side _____ an ___ an-gel like you.

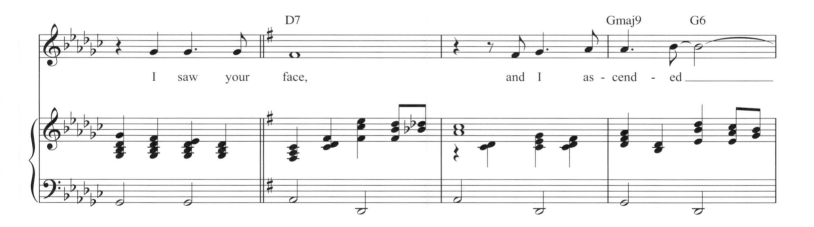

I saw your face, and I as - cend - ed _____

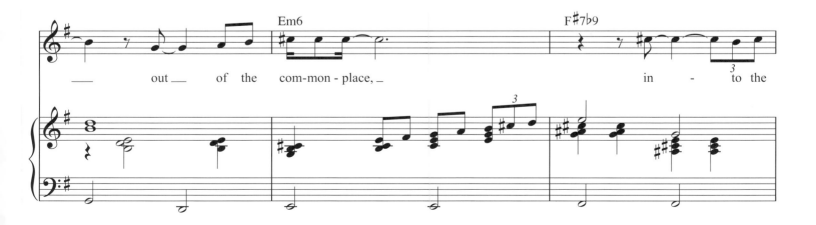

___ out ___ of the com-mon - place, _ in - to the

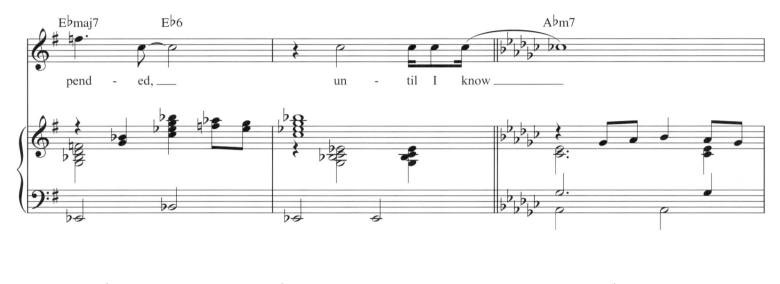

rare. _____ Some-where _ in space, I hang sus-

pend - ed, ___ un - til I know _____

there's a chance _ that you care. Won't you an - swer this fer - vent prayer

rit. *a tempo*

of a stran - ger in par - a - dise? _____ Don't ___ send me _

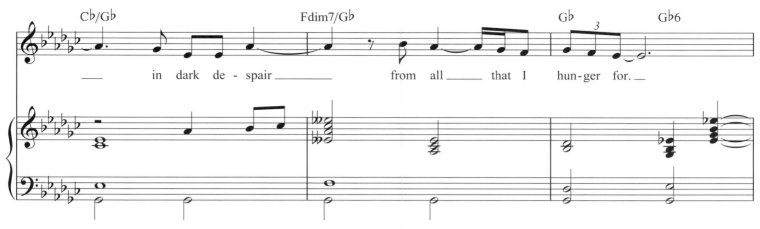

in dark de-spair _____ from all ____ that I hun-ger for. __

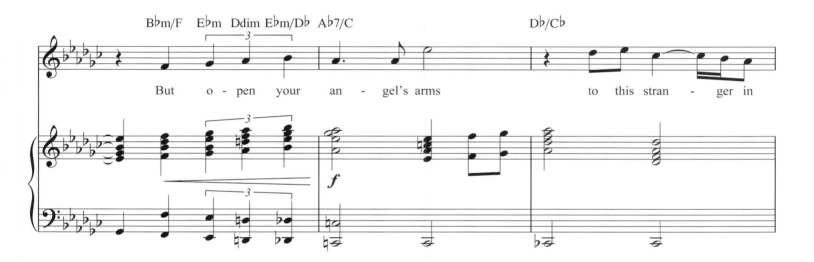

But o-pen your an - gel's arms to this stran - ger in

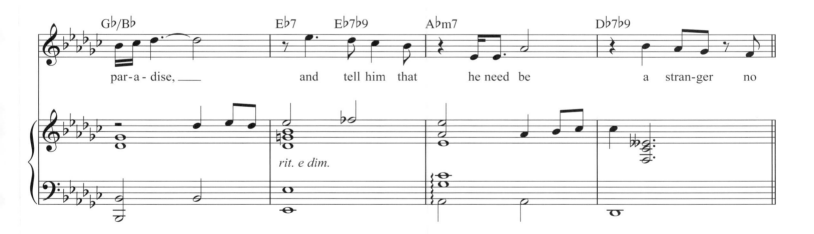

par-a-dise, ___ and tell him that he need be a stran-ger no

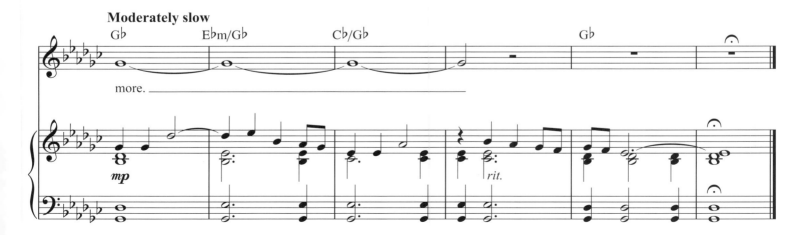

Moderately slow

more. _____

TAKE THE "A" TRAIN/DON'T GET AROUND MUCH ANYMORE

TAKE THE "A" TRAIN
Words and Music by BILLY STRAYHORN

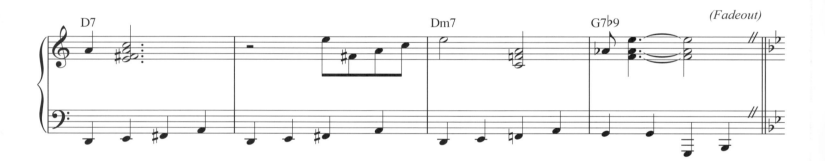

DON'T GET AROUND MUCH ANYMORE
Words and Music by DUKE ELLINGTON and BOB RUSSELL

take a book down _ from the shelf. And what with pro - grams

on the air, I keep pret-ty much to my - self. Missed the Sat - ur - day dance. _

Moderately slow Swing

Heard they crowd-ed the floor. _

Could-n't bear it with-out you. Don't get a - round much an - y - more. _

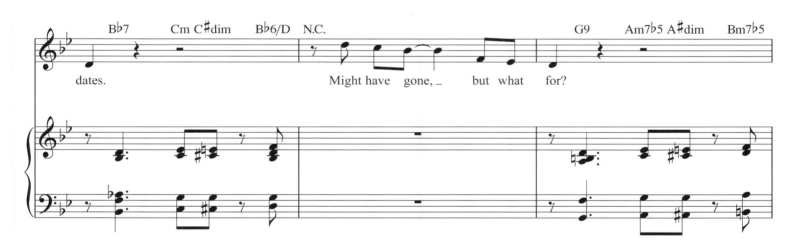

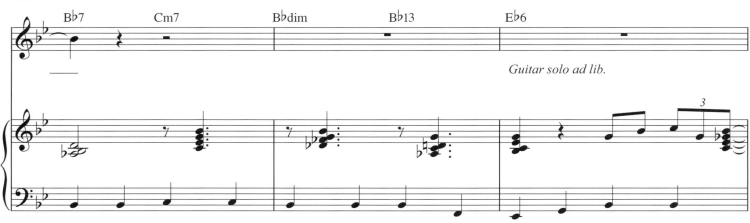

Guitar solo ad lib.

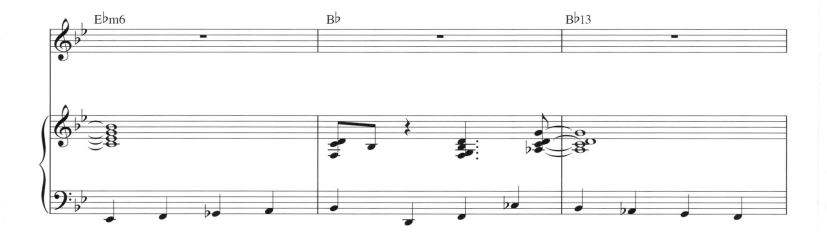

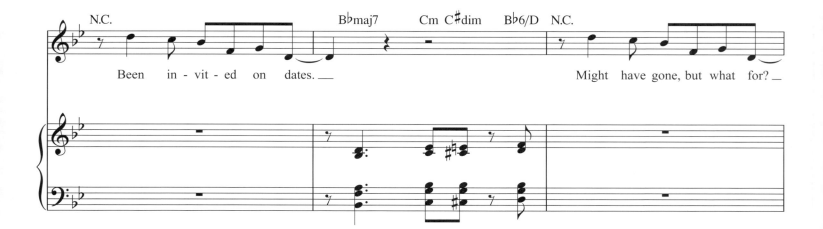

Been in-vit-ed on dates. __ Might have gone, but what for? __

WHO CAN I TURN TO
(When Nobody Needs Me)
from THE ROAR OF THE GREASEPAINT - THE SMELL OF THE CROWD

Words and Music by LESLIE BRICUSSE
and ANTHONY NEWLEY

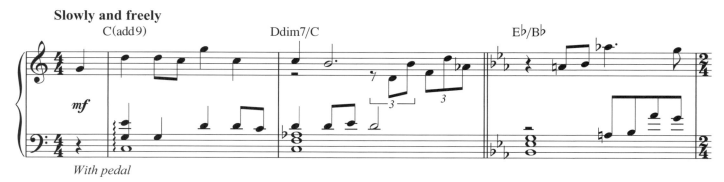

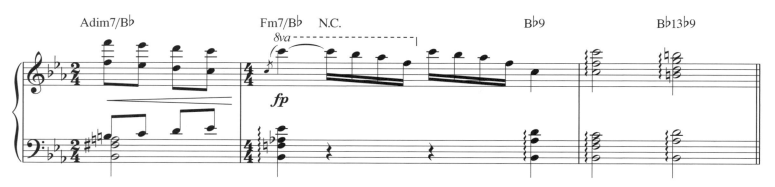

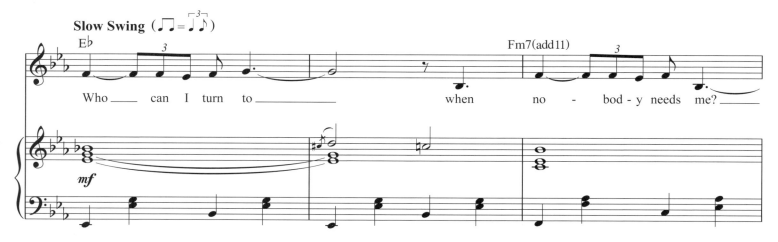

Who ___ can I turn to ___ when no - bod - y needs me?

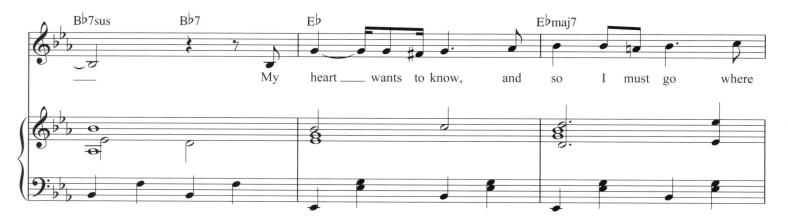

___ My heart ___ wants to know, and so I must go where

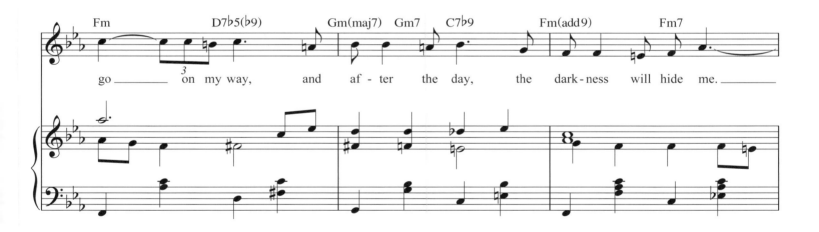

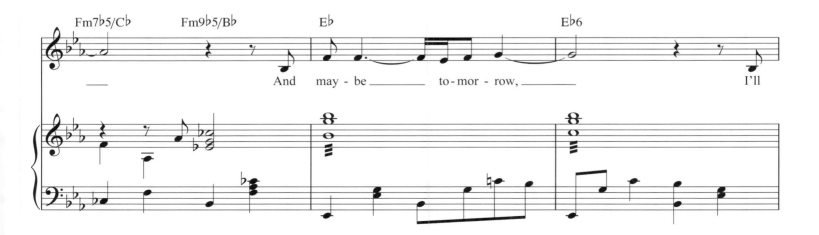

find ____ what I'm af - ter. _____ I'll throw ____ off my sor - row, ____

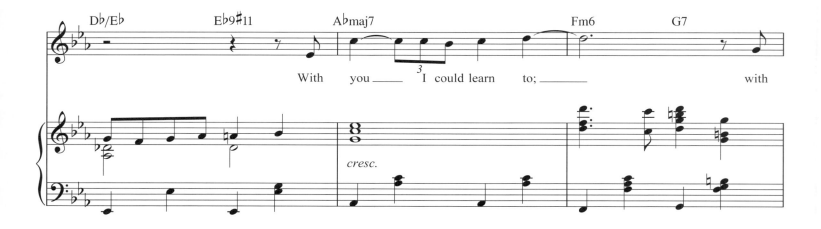

beg, steal or bor - row my share of laugh - ter.

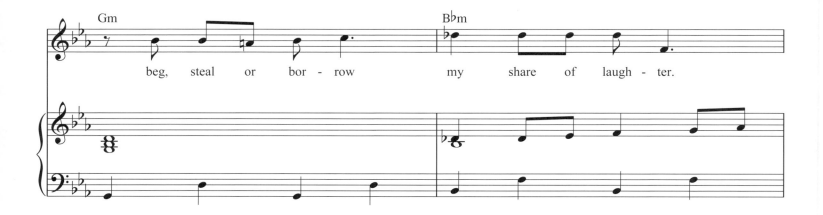

With you ____ I could learn to; _____ with

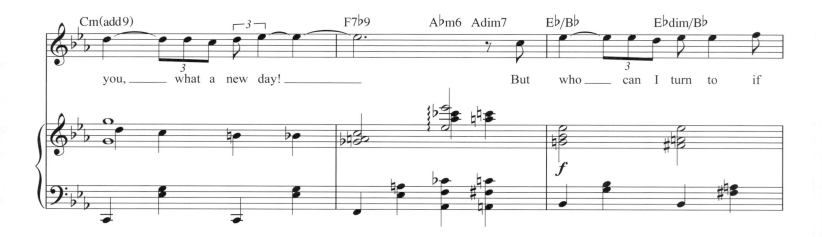

you, ____ what a new day! _____ But who ____ can I turn to if

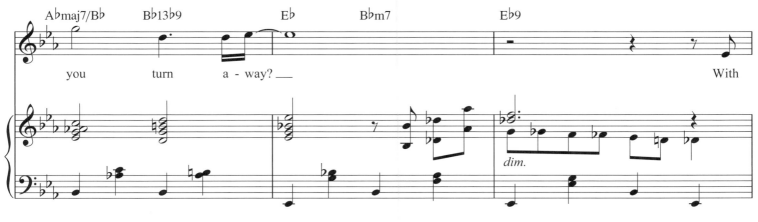

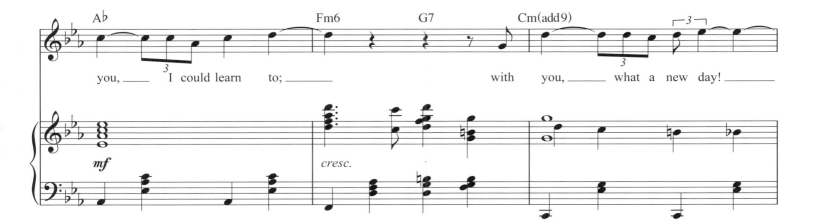

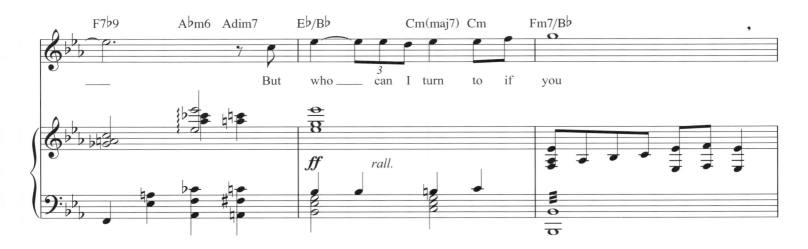

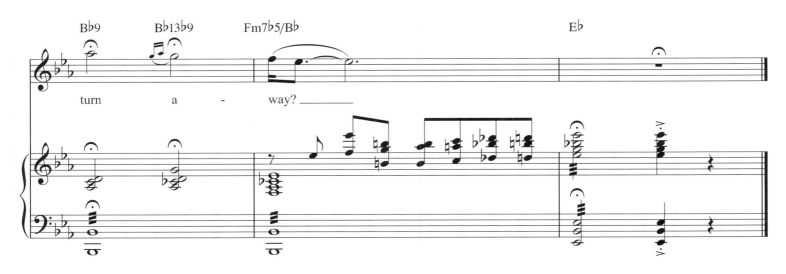

WHERE DO I BEGIN
(Love Theme)
from the Paramount Picture LOVE STORY

Words by CARL SIGMAN
Music by FRANCIS LAI

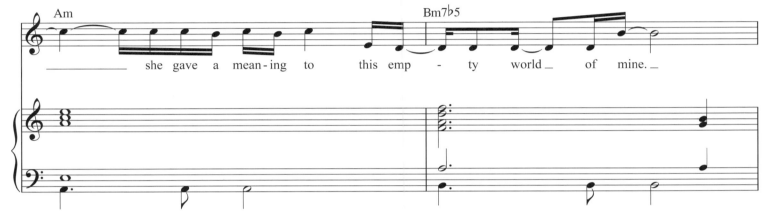

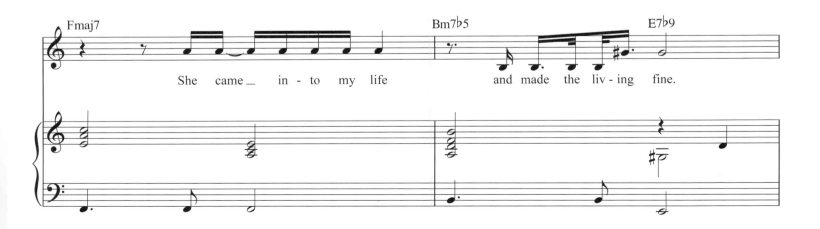

She fills my heart. _____ She fills _ my heart _

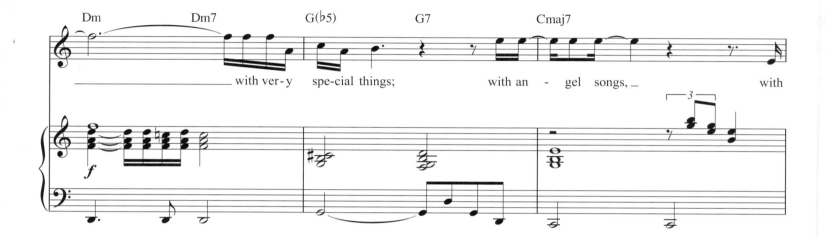

_____ with ver-y spe-cial things; with an - gel songs, _ with

wild im - ag - in - ings. She fills ___ my soul ___ with so much

love, that an - y-where I go, _____ I'm nev-er lone - ly. With her a -

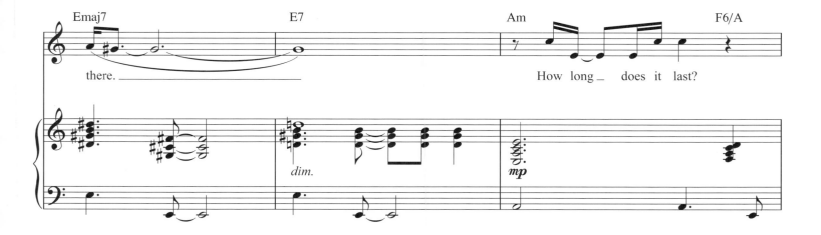

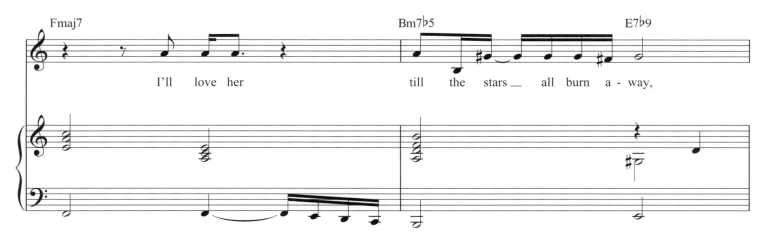

I'll love her till the stars all burn a - way,

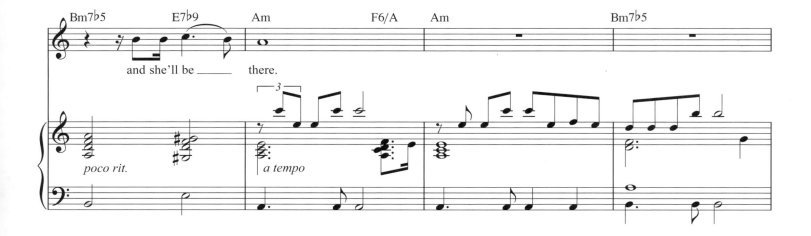

and she'll be there.

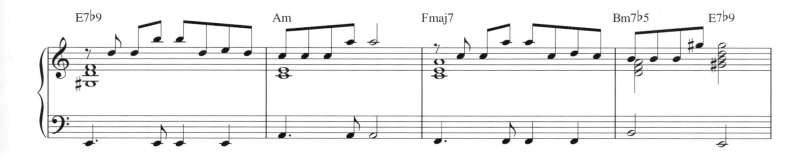

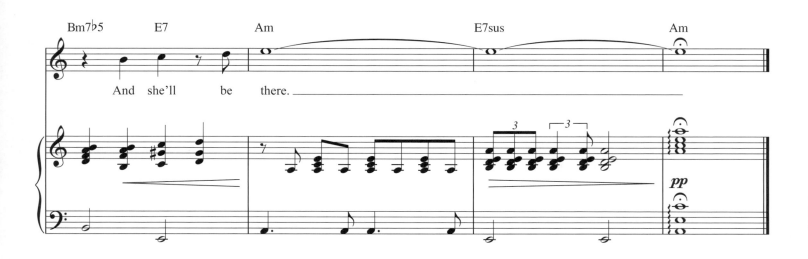

And she'll be there.